THE MERCHANT OF VENICE

THE MERCHANT OF VENICE

WILLIAM SHAKESPEARE

Illustrated in Color by
SIR JAMES D. LINTON

Illustrated in Black and White by
SIR JOHN GILBERT

GRAMERCY BOOKS
NEW YORK • AVENEL

Preface and Compilation
Copyright © 1994 by Outlet Book Company, Inc.

This edition is published by Gramercy Books
distributed by Outlet Book Company, Inc.,
a Random House Company,
40 Engelhard Avenue
Avenel, New Jersey 07001

The text used in this edition was
originally published in
The New Temple Shakespeare series,
edited by M.R. Ridley

Designed by Melissa Ring

Random House
New York • Toronto • London • Sydney • Auckland

Printed and bound in Singapore

Library of Congress Cataloging-in-Publication Data

8 7 6 5 4 3 2 1

PREFACE

William Shakespeare probably wrote *The Merchant of Venice* in 1596 or 1597, and it is a superb example of his ability to adapt and transform little more than anecdotes into a new and dramatically effective play. The plot of *The Merchant of Venice* is based on two folktales of indeterminate age and origin that Shakespeare was said to have acquired from Italian sources. The first is the story of the creditor who demands a pound of flesh in payment of a defaulted debt. The other is the story of the lover who must choose among three caskets in a riddle game to win the hand of a wealthy lady. From these two disparate tales Shakespeare constructs a marvelous and elaborate whole, one of his most memorable comedies peopled by some of his most unforgettable characters.

Christopher Marlowe's popular play, *The Jew of Malta*, also influenced Shakespeare's writing of *The Merchant of Venice*. In Marlowe's usurious Barabas, Shakespeare found the prototype for Shylock, the moneylender. But where Barabas was a brilliant caricature of Machiavellian evil, Shylock is a character of all too human frailty and complexity. He is one of Shakespeare's great creations and a major reason for the play's perennial popularity with audiences. Actors, too, have always been drawn to the part of Shylock, and interpretations have ranged from depictions of an avaricious, comic villain to a sympathetic, wronged man.

The play also includes one of Shakespeare's greatest heroines—Portia. She is a young noblewoman who lives in the wealthy splendor of idyllic Belmont across the sea from Venice.

She is both wise and virtuous, but her goodness goes beyond mere sentiment. She is also, when necessary, a woman of initiative and resolute action. When Antonio, her husband Bassanio's friend, is in mortal danger from Shylock she is quick to come to his aid. In the play's great climactic courtroom scene it is Portia, disguised as a man, who, with a clever and learned argument, is able to deliver Antonio from Shylock's vengeful knife.

The Merchant of Venice is certainly one of Shakespeare's most enjoyable and finely wrought comedies. With its rich characterizations and its evocative storylines, the scenes move deftly from high comedy to tense drama to romantic lyricism and radiate a dramatic mastery that can only be called Shakespearean.

Shakespeare's plays were first published individually, in Quarto editions. Later they were collected and published in Folio editions. There are often variations in the text from edition to edition. The text of this edition of *The Merchant of Venice* is the nearest possible approximation to what Shakespeare actually wrote and is based on the earliest reliable printed texts. To avoid distraction, however, the spelling has been modernized. Where a Quarto text exists as well as the First Folio, the passages which occur only in the Quarto are enclosed in square brackets and those which occur only in the Folio are enclosed in brace brackets. The punctuation adheres closely to the Elizabethan punctuation of the early texts and, therefore, is often indicative of the way in which the lines are to be spoken.

This handsome edition of *The Merchant of Venice* is illustrated by Sir James D. Linton, who artfully captures the sumptuous world of Renaissance Venice.

CHRISTOPHER MOORE

New York
1994

DRAMATIS PERSONAE

THE DUKE OF VENICE.
THE PRINCE OF MOROCCO,⎫ *suitors to Portia.*
THE PRINCE OF ARRAGON, ⎭
ANTONIO, *a merchant of Venice.*
BASSANIO, *his friend, suitor to Portia.*
SOLANIO, ⎫
GRATIANO, ⎬ *friends to Antonio and Bassanio.*
SALERIO, ⎭
LORENZO, *in love with Jessica.*
SHYLOCK, *a rich Jew.*
TUBAL, *a Jew, his friend.*
LAUNCELOT GOBBO, *the clown, servant to Shylock.*
OLD GOBBO, *father to Launcelot.*
LEONARDO, *servant to Bassanio.*
BALTHASAR,⎫ *servants to Portia.*
STEPHANO, ⎭

PORTIA, *a rich heiress.*
NERISSA, *her waiting-maid.*
JESSICA, *daughter to Shylock.*

Magnificoes of Venice, Officers of the Court of Justice,
Gaoler, Servants to Portia, and other Attendants.

SCENE: *Partly at Venice, and partly at Belmont,*
the seat of Portia.

ACT I

SCENE I

Venice. A street

Enter Antonio, Salerio, and Solanio

Antonio. In sooth, I know not why I am so sad,
  It wearies me, you say it wearies you;
  But how I caught it, found it, or came by it,
  What stuff 'tis made of, whereof it is born,
  I am to learn;
  And such a want-wit sadness makes of me,
  That I have much ado to know myself.
Salerio. Your mind is tossing on the ocean,
  There where your argosies with portly sail,
  Like signiors and rich burghers on the flood,
  Or as it were the pageants of the sea,
  Do overpeer the petty traffickers,
  That curt'sy to them, do them reverence,
  As they fly by them with their woven wings.
Solanio. Believe me, sir, had I such venture forth,
  The better part of my affections would
  Be with my hopes abroad. I should be still
  Plucking the grass to know where sits the wind,
  Piring in maps for ports, and piers, and roads;
  And every object that might make me fear
  Misfortune to my ventures, out of doubt
  Would make me sad.
Salerio.   My wind, cooling my broth,
  Would blow me to an ague, when I thought
  What harm a wind too great might do at sea.

I should not see the sandy hour-glass run
But I should think of shallows and of flats,
And see, my wealthy Andrew docks in sand
Vailing her high top lower than her ribs
To kiss her burial. Should I go to church
And see the holy edifice of stone,
And not bethink me straight of dangerous
    rocks,
Which touching but my gentle vessel's side
Would scatter all her spices on the stream,
Enrobe the roaring waters with my silks,
And, in a word, but even now worth this,
And now worth nothing? Shall I have the
    thought
To think on this, and shall I lack the thought
That such a thing bechanc'd would make me
    sad?
But tell not me, I know Antonio
Is sad to think upon his merchandise.
Antonio. Believe me, no; I thank my fortune for
    it,
My ventures are not in one bottom trusted,
Nor to one place; nor is my whole estate
Upon the fortune of this present year:
Therefore my merchandise makes me not sad.
Solanio. Why then, you are in love.
Antonio.   Fie, fie!
Solanio. Not in love neither? Then let us say you
    are sad
  Because you are not merry; and 'twere as easy
  For you to laugh and leap, and say you are
    merry
  Because you are not sad. Now, by two-headed
    Janus,
  Nature hath fram'd strange fellows in her time:

Some that will evermore peep through their
eyes,
And laugh like parrots at a bag-piper;
And other of such vinegar aspect,
That they'll not show their teeth in way of
smile,
Though Nestor swear the jest be laughable.

Enter Bassanio, Lorenzo, and Gratiano

Here comes Bassanio, your most noble kins-
man,
Gratiano, and Lorenzo. Fare ye well,
We leave you now with better company.
Salerio. I would have stay'd till I had made you
merry,
If worthier friends had not prevented me.
Antonio. Your worth is very dear in my regard.
I take it your own business calls on you,
And you embrace the occasion to depart.
Salerio. Good morrow, my good lords.
Bassanio. Good signiors both, when shall we
laugh? say, when?
You grow exceeding strange: must it be so?
Salerio. We'll make our leisures to attend on yours.
Exeunt Salerio and Solanio
Lorenzo. My Lord Bassanio, since you have
found Antonio,
We two will leave you, but at dinner-time
I pray you have in mind where we must meet.
Bassanio. I will not fail you.
Gratiano. You look not well, Signior Antonio,
You have too much respect upon the world:
They lose it that do buy it with much care,
Believe me, you are marvellously chang'd.
Antonio. I hold the world but as the world, Gra-
tiano,

A stage, where every man must play a part,
And mine a sad one.
Gratiano.   Let me play the fool,
With mirth and laughter let old wrinkles come,
And let my liver rather heat with wine
Than my heart cool with mortifying groans.
Why should a man whose blood is warm within
Sit like his grandsire, cut in alabaster?
Sleep when he wakes? and creep into the jaun-
   dice
By being peevish? I tell thee what, Antonio,
I love thee, and it is my love that speaks:
There are a sort of men, whose visages
Do cream and mantle like a standing pond,
And do a wilful stillness entertain,
With purpose to be dress'd in an opinion
Of wisdom, gravity, profound conceit,
As who should say, 'I am Sir Oracle,
And when I ope my lips, let no dog bark!'
O my Antonio, I do know of these
That therefore only are reputed wise
For saying nothing; when I am very sure
If they should speak, would almost damn
   those ears,
Which, hearing them, would call their brothers
   fools.
I'll tell thee more of this another time.
But fish not with this melancholy bait
For this fool gudgeon, this opinion.
Come, good Lorenzo, fare ye well awhile;
I'll end my exhortation after dinner.
Lorenzo. Well, we will leave you then till dinner-
   time:
I must be one of these same dumb wise men,
For Gratiano never lets me speak.

Gratiano. Well, keep me company but two years
  moe,
 Thou shalt not know the sound of thine own
  tongue.
Antonio. Fare you well, I'll grow a talker for this
  gear.
Gratiano. Thanks, i' faith, for silence is only
  commendable
 In a neat's tongue dried, and a maid not ven-
  dible.   *Exeunt Gratiano and Lorenzo*
Antonio. Is that any thing now?
Bassanio. Gratiano speaks an infinite deal of noth-
  ing more than any man in all Venice; his rea-
  sons are as two grains of wheat hid in two
  bushels of chaff; you shall seek all day ere you
  find them, and when you have them, they
  are not worth the search.
Antonio. Well, tell me now what lady is the same
 To whom you swore a secret pilgrimage,
 That you to-day promis'd to tell me of.
Bassanio. 'Tis not unknown to you, Antonio,
 How much I have disabled mine estate,
 By something showing a more swelling port
 Than my faint means would grant continu-
  ance:
 Nor do I now make moan to be abridg'd
 From such a noble rate, but my chief care
 Is to come fairly off from the great debts
 Wherein my time, something too prodigal,
 Half left me gag'd. To you, Antonio,
 I owe the most in money and in love,
 And from your love I have a warranty
 To unburthen all my plots and purposes
 How to get clear of all the debts I owe.

Antonio. I pray you, good Bassanio, let me know
    it,
    And if it stand, as you yourself still do,
    Within the eye of honour, be assur'd,
    My purse, my person, my extremest means,
    Lie all unlock'd to your occasions.
Bassanio. In my school-days, when I had lost one
    shaft,
    I shot his fellow of the self-same flight
    The self-same way, with more advised watch,
    To find the other forth, and by adventuring
    both,
    I oft found both: I urge this childhood proof,
    Because what follows is pure innocence.
    I owe you much, and like a wilful youth
    That which I owe is lost, but if you please
    To shoot another arrow that self way
    Which you did shoot the first, I do not doubt,
    As I will watch the aim, or to find both,
    Or bring your latter hazard back again,
    And thankfully rest debtor for the first.
Antonio. You know me well, and herein spend
    but time
    To wind about my love with circumstance,
    And out of doubt you do me now more wrong
    In making question of my uttermost,
    Than if you had made waste of all I have:
    Then do but say to me what I should do
    That in your knowledge may by me be done,
    And I am prest unto it: therefore speak.
Bassanio. In Belmont is a lady richly left,
    And she is fair, and fairer than that word,
    Of wondrous virtues; sometimes from her eyes
    I did receive fair speechless messages:
    Her name is Portia, nothing undervalued
    To Cato's daughter, Brutus' Portia,

Nor is the wide world ignorant of her worth,
For the four winds blow in from every coast
Renowned suitors, and her sunny locks
Hang on her temples like a golden fleece,
Which makes her seat of Belmont Colchos'
    strond,
And many Jasons come in quest of her.
O my Antonio, had I but the means
To hold a rival place with one of them,
I have a mind presages me such thrift,
That I should questionless be fortunate!
Antonio. Thou know'st that all my fortunes are at
    sea,
Neither have I money, nor commodity
To raise a present sum; therefore go forth,
Try what my credit can in Venice do,
That shall be rack'd even to the uttermost
To furnish thee to Belmont to fair Portia.
Go, presently inquire, and so will I,
Where money is, and I no question make
To have it of my trust, or for my sake.   *Exeunt*

SCENE II

Belmont. A room in Portia's house

Enter Portia and Nerissa

Portia. By my troth, Nerissa, my little body is aweary of this great world.

Nerissa. You would be, sweet madam, if your miseries were in the same abundance as your good fortunes are: and yet, for aught I see, they are as sick that surfeit with too much, as they that starve with nothing; it is no mean happiness therefore to be seated in the mean; superfluity comes sooner by white hairs, but competency lives longer.

Portia. Good sentences, and well pronounc'd.

Nerissa. They would be better if well followed.

Portia. If to do were as easy as to know what were good to do, chapels had been churches, and poor men's cottages princes' palaces; it is a good divine that follows his own instructions, I can easier teach twenty what were good to be done, than to be one of the twenty to follow mine own teaching: the brain may devise laws for the blood, but a hot temper leaps o'er a cold decree, such a hare is madness the youth, to skip o'er the meshes of good counsel the cripple; but this reasoning is not in the fashion to choose me a husband——O me, the word 'choose'! I may neither choose who I

would, nor refuse who I dislike, so is the will of a living daughter curb'd by the will of a dead father: is it not hard, Nerissa, that I cannot choose one, nor refuse none?

Nerissa. Your father was ever virtuous, and holy men at their death have good inspirations; therefore the lottery that he hath devised in these three chests of gold, silver, and lead, whereof who chooses his meaning chooses you, will no doubt never be chosen by any rightly, but one who you shall rightly love. But what warmth is there in your affection towards any of these princely suitors that are already come?

Portia. I pray thee over-name them, and as thou namest them, I will describe them; and according to my description level at my affection.

Nerissa. First there is the Neapolitan prince.

Portia. Ay, that's a colt indeed, for he doth nothing but talk of his horse, and he makes it a great appropriation to his own good parts that he can shoe him himself; I am much afear'd my lady his mother play'd false with a smith.

Nerissa. Then there is the County Palatine.

Portia. He doth nothing but frown; (as who should say, 'an you will not have me, choose,' he hears merry tales and smiles not; I fear he will prove the weeping philosopher when he grows old, being so full of unmannerly sadness in his youth.) I had rather be married to a death's-head with a bone in his mouth, than to either of these. God defend me from these two!

Nerissa. How say you by the French lord, Monsieur Le Bon?

Portia. God made him, and therefore let him pass

for a man; in truth I know it is a sin to be a mocker, but he!—why, he hath a horse better than the Neapolitan's, a better bad habit of frowning than the Count Palatine, he is every man in no man, if a throstle sing, he falls straight a capering, he will fence with his own shadow: if I should marry him, I should marry twenty husbands: if he would despise me, I would forgive him, for if he love me to madness, I shall never requite him.

Nerissa. What say you, then, to Falconbridge, the young baron of England?

Portia. You know I say nothing to him, for he understands not me, nor I him: he hath neither Latin, French, nor Italian, and you will come into the court and swear that I have a poor pennyworth in the English: he is a proper man's picture, but alas, who can converse with a dumb-show? How oddly he is suited! I think he bought his doublet in Italy, his round hose in France, his bonnet in Germany, and his behaviour every where.

Nerissa. What think you of the Scottish lord, his neighbour?

Portia. That he hath a neighbourly charity in him, for he borrowed a box of the ear of the Englishman, and swore he would pay him again when he was able: I think the Frenchman became his surety, and seal'd under for another.

Nerissa. How like you the young German, the Duke of Saxony's nephew?

Portia. Very vilely in the morning when he is sober, and most vilely in the afternoon when he is drunk: when he is best, he is a little worse

than a man, and when he is worst, he is little
better than a beast: an the worst fall that ever
fell, I hope I shall make shift to go without
him.

Nerissa. If he should offer to choose, and choose
the right casket, you should refuse to perform
your father's will, if you should refuse to accept him.

Portia. Therefore, for fear of the worst, I pray
thee set a deep glass of Rhenish wine on the
contrary casket, for if the devil be within, and
that temptation without, I know he will choose
it. I will do any thing, Nerissa, ere I will be
married to a sponge.

Nerissa. You need not fear, lady, the having any
of these lords: they have acquainted me with
their determinations, which is indeed to return
to their home, and to trouble you with no more
suit, unless you may be won by some other sort
than your father's imposition, depending on the
caskets.

Portia. If I live to be as old as Sibylla, I will die
as chaste as Diana, unless I be obtained by the
manner of my father's will. I am glad this par-
cel of wooers are so reasonable, for there is
not one among them but I dote on his very absence; and I pray God grant them a fair de-
parture.

Nerissa. Do you not remember, lady, in your
father's time, a Venetian, a scholar and a sol-
dier, that came hither in company of the Mar-
quis of Montferrat?

Portia. Yes, yes, it was Bassanio; as I think so was
he call'd.

Nerissa. True, madam, he of all the men that ever my foolish eyes look'd upon, was the best deserving a fair lady.

Portia. I remember him well, and I remember him worthy of thy praise.

Enter a Serving-man

How now, what news?

Serving-man. The four strangers seek for you, madam, to take their leave: and there is a forerunner come from a fifth, the Prince of Morocco, who brings word the prince his master will be here to-night.

Portia. If I could bid the fifth welcome with so good heart as I can bid the other four farewell, I should be glad of his approach: if he have the condition of a saint, and the complexion of a devil, I had rather he should shrive me than wive me.

Come, Nerissa. Sirrah, go before.

Whiles we shut the gate upon one wooer, another knocks at the door. *Exeunt*

SCENE III

Venice. A public place

Enter Bassanio and Shylock

Shylock. Three thousand ducats, well.

Bassanio. Ay, sir, for three months.

Shylock. For three months, well.

Bassanio. For the which, as I told you, Antonio shall be bound.

Shylock. Antonio shall become bound, well.

Bassanio. May you stead me? will you pleasure me? shall I know your answer?

Shylock. Three thousand ducats for three months, and Antonio bound.

Bassanio. Your answer to that.

Shylock. Antonio is a good man.

Bassanio. Have you heard any imputation to the contrary?

Shylock. Ho, no, no, no, no: my meaning in saying he is a good man, is to have you understand me that he is sufficient, yet his means are in supposition: he hath an argosy bound to Tripolis, another to the Indies, I understand moreover upon the Rialto, he hath a third at Mexico, a fourth for England, and other ventures he hath squander'd abroad; but ships are but boards, sailors but men, there be land-rats, and water-rats, water-thieves, and land-thieves, I mean pirates, and then there is the peril of waters, winds, and rocks: the man is notwithstanding sufficient; three thousand ducats, I think I may take his bond.

Bassanio. Be assur'd you may.

Shylock. I will be assur'd I may; and that I may be assur'd, I will bethink me; may I speak with Antonio?

Bassanio. If it please you to dine with us.

Shylock. Yes, to smell pork, to eat of the habitation which your prophet the Nazarite conjured the devil into: I will buy with you, sell with you, talk with you, walk with you, and so following: but I will not eat with you, drink with you, nor pray with you. What news on the Rialto? Who is he comes here?

Enter Antonio

Bassanio. This is Signior Antonio.

Shylock. (*aside*) How like a fawning publican he looks!
I hate him for he is a Christian;
But more, for that in low simplicity
He lends out money gratis, and brings down
The rate of usance here with us in Venice.
If I can catch him once upon the hip,
I will feed fat the ancient grudge I bear him.
He hates our sacred nation, and he rails,
Even there where merchants most do congregate,
On me, my bargains, and my well-won thrift,
Which he calls interest. Cursed be my tribe
If I forgive him!

Bassanio.   Shylock, do you hear?

Shylock. I am debating of my present store,
And by the near guess of my memory
I cannot instantly raise up the gross
Of full three thousand ducats: what of that?
Tubal, a wealthy Hebrew of my tribe,
Will furnish me. But soft! how many months
Do you desire? (*to Antonio*) Rest you fair, good signior,
Your worship was the last man in our mouths.

Antonio. Shylock, albeit I neither lend nor borrow
By taking nor by giving of excess,

Yet, to supply the ripe wants of my friend,
I'll break a custom. Is he yet possess'd
How much ye would?
Shylock.   Ay, ay, three thousand ducats.
Antonio. And for three months.
Shylock. I had forgot, three months, you told me
    so.
    Well then, your bond; and let me see, but hear
    you,
    Methoughts you said you neither lend nor
    borrow
    Upon advantage.
Antonio.   I do never use it.
Shylock. When Jacob graz'd his uncle Laban's
    sheep,—
    This Jacob from our holy Abram was
    (As his wise mother wrought in his behalf)
    The third possessor; ay, he was the third,—
Antonio. And what of him? did he take interest?
Shylock. No, not take interest, not, as you would
    say,
    Directly interest: mark what Jacob did.
    When Laban and himself were compromis'd
    That all the eanlings which were streak'd and
    pied
    Should fall as Jacob's hire, the ewes being rank
    In end of autumn turned to the rams,
    And when the work of generation was
    Between these woolly breeders in the act,
    The skilful shepherd pill'd me certain wands,
    And in the doing of the deed of kind
    He stuck them up before the fulsome ewes,
    Who, then conceiving, did in eaning time
    Fall parti-colour'd lambs, and those were
    Jacob's.
    This was a way to thrive, and he was blest:
    And thrift is blessing if men steal it not.

Antonio. This was a venture, sir, that Jacob serv'd
  for;
  A thing not in his power to bring to pass,
  But sway'd and fashion'd by the hand of
    heaven.
  Was this inserted to make interest good?
  Or is your gold and silver ewes and rams?
Shylock. I cannot tell; I make it breed as fast:
  But note me, signior.
Antonio.   Mark you this, Bassanio,
  The devil can cite Scripture for his purpose,
  An evil soul producing holy witness
  Is like a villain with a smiling cheek,
  A goodly apple rotten at the heart:
  O, what a goodly outside falsehood hath!
Shylock. Three thousand ducats, 'tis a good round
    sum.
  Three months from twelve; then, let me see,
    the rate—
Antonio. Well, Shylock, shall we be beholding to
    you?
Shylock. Signior Antonio, many a time and oft
  In the Rialto you have rated me
  About my moneys and my usances:
  Still have I borne it with a patient shrug,
  (For sufferance is the badge of all our tribe).
  You call me misbeliever, cut-throat dog,
  And spit upon my Jewish gaberdine,
  And all for use of that which is mine own.
  Well then, it now appears you need my help:
  Go to then, you come to me, and you say,
  'Shylock, we would have moneys:' you say so,
  You that did void your rheum upon my beard,
  And foot me as you spurn a stranger cur
  Over your threshold, moneys is your suit.
  What should I say to you? Should I not say
  'Hath a dog money? is it possible

A cur can lend three thousand ducats?' or
Shall I bend low, and in a bondman's key,
With bated breath, and whispering humble-
    ness,
Say this,—
'Fair sir, you spit on me on Wednesday last,
You spurn'd me such a day, another time
You call'd me dog; and for these courtesies
I'll lend you thus much moneys'?

Antonio. I am as like to call thee so again,
To spit on thee again, to spurn thee too.
If thou wilt lend this money, lend it not
As to thy friends, for when did friendship take
A breed for barren metal of his friend?
But lend it rather to thine enemy,
Who if he break, thou may'st with better face
Exact the penalty.

Shylock.   Why, look you how you storm!
I would be friends with you, and have your
    love,
Forget the shames that you have stain'd me
    with,
Supply your present wants, and take no doit
Of usance for my moneys, and you'll not hear
    me:
This is kind I offer.

Bassanio. This were kindness.

Shylock.   This kindness will I show;
Go with me to a notary, seal me there
Your single bond, and, in a merry sport,
If you repay me not on such a day,
In such a place, such sum or sums as are
Express'd in the condition, let the forfeit
Be nominated for an equal pound
Of your fair flesh, to be cut off and taken
In what part of your body pleaseth me.

Antonio. Content, i' faith, I'll seal to such a bond,

And say there is much kindness in the Jew.

Bassanio. You shall not seal to such a bond for me,

I'll rather dwell in my necessity.

Antonio. Why, fear not, man, I will not forfeit it;

Within these two months, that's a month before

This bond expires, I do expect return

Of thrice three times the value of this bond.

Shylock. O father Abram, what these Christians are,

Whose own hard dealings teaches them suspect

The thoughts of others! Pray you, tell me this,

If he should break his day, what should I gain

By the exaction of the forfeiture?

A pound of man's flesh taken from a man

Is not so estimable, profitable neither,

As flesh of muttons, beefs, or goats. I say,

To buy his favour, I extend this friendship;

If he will take it, so, if not, adieu,

And, for my love, I pray you wrong me not.

Antonio. Yes, Shylock, I will seal unto this bond.

Shylock. Then meet me forthwith at the notary's,

Give him direction for this merry bond,

And I will go and purse the ducats straight,

See to my house, left in the fearful guard

Of an unthrifty knave; and presently

I'll be with you.

Antonio.   Hie thee, gentle Jew.

Exit Shylock

The Hebrew will turn Christian, he grows kind.

Bassanio. I like not fair terms, and a villain's mind.

Antonio. Come on, in this there can be no dismay,

My ships come home a month before the day.

Exeunt

ACT II

SCENE I

Belmont. A room in Portia's house

Flourish of cornets. Enter the Prince of Morocco, a tawny Moor all in white, and three or four followers accordingly, with Portia, Nerissa, and their train

Morocco. Mislike me not for my complexion,
  The shadowed livery of the burnish'd sun,
  To whom I am a neighbour, and near bred.
  Bring me the fairest creature northward born,
  Where Phœbus' fire scarce thaws the icicles,
  And let us make incision for your love,
  To prove whose blood is reddest, his or mine.
  I tell thee, lady, this aspect of mine
  Hath fear'd the valiant: by my love, I swear
  The best-regarded virgins of our clime
  Hath lov'd it too: I would not change this hue,
  Except to steal your thoughts, my gentle
    queen.
Portia. In terms of choice I am not solely led
  By nice direction of a maiden's eyes;
  Besides, the lottery of my destiny
  Bars me the right of voluntary choosing:
  But if my father had not scanted me,
  And hedg'd me by his wit to yield myself
  His wife, who wins me by that means I told
    you,
  Yourself, renowned prince, then stood as fair
  As any comer I have look'd on yet
  For my affection.

Morocco.   Even for that I thank you;
  Therefore I pray you lead me to the caskets
  To try my fortune. By this scimitar
  That slew the Sophy, and a Persian prince
  That won three fields of Sultan Solyman,
  I would outstare the sternest eyes that look,
  Outbrave the heart most daring on the earth,
  Pluck the young sucking cubs from the she-
      bear,
  Yea, mock the lion when he roars for prey,
  To win thee, lady. But, alas the while,
  If Hercules and Lichas play at dice
  Which is the better man, the greater throw
  May turn by fortune from the weaker hand:
  So is Alcides beaten by his page,
  And so may I, blind fortune leading me,
  Miss that which one unworthier may attain,
  And die with grieving.
Portia.   You must take your chance,
  And either not attempt to choose at all,
  Or swear before you choose, if you choose
      wrong,
  Never to speak to lady afterward
  In way of marriage; therefore be advis'd.
Morocco. Nor will not, come, bring me unto my
      chance.
Portia. First forward to the temple; after dinner
  Your hazard shall be made.
Morocco.   Good fortune then,
  To make me blest or cursed'st among men!
                    Cornets, and exeunt

SCENE II

Venice. A street

Enter Launcelot

Launcelot. Certainly, my conscience will serve
me to run from this Jew my master: the fiend is
at mine elbow, and tempts me, saying to me,
'Gobbo, Launcelot Gobbo, good Launcelot,'
or 'good Gobbo,' or 'good Launcelot Gobbo,
use your legs, take the start, run away;' my
conscience says, 'No; take heed, honest
Launcelot, take heed, honest Gobbo,' or, as
aforesaid, 'honest Launcelot Gobbo, do not
run, scorn running with thy heels.' Well, the
the most courageous fiend bids me pack, 'Via!'
says the fiend, 'away!' says the fiend, 'for the
heavens, rouse up a brave mind,' says the
fiend, 'and run.' Well, my conscience, hanging
about the neck of my heart, says very wisely to
me, 'My honest friend Launcelot, being an
honest man's son,'—or rather an honest
woman's son;—for, indeed, my father did something smack, something grow to—he had a kind
of taste;—well, my conscience says, 'Launcelot,
budge not,' 'budge,' says the fiend, 'budge not,'
says my conscience, 'conscience,' say I, 'you
counsel well,' 'fiend,' say I, 'you counsel well:'
to be rul'd by my conscience, I should stay
with the Jew my master, who, God bless the

mark, is a kind of devil; and, to run away from the Jew, I should be ruled by the fiend, who, saving your reverence, is the devil himself. Certainly the Jew is the very devil incarnation, and, in my conscience, my conscience is but a kind of hard conscience, to offer to counsel me to stay with the Jew; the fiend gives the more friendly counsel: I will run, fiend, my heels are at your commandment, I will run.

Enter Old Gobbo, with a basket

Gobbo. Master young-man, you, I pray you, which is the way to master Jew's?

Launcelot. (*aside*) O heavens, this is my true-begotten father, who, being more than sand-blind, high-gravel blind, knows me not, I will try confusions with him.

Gobbo. Master young gentleman, I pray you which is the way to master Jew's?

Launcelot. Turn up on your right hand at the next turning, but at the next turning of all on your left; marry, at the very next turning, turn of no hand, but turn down indirectly to the Jew's house.

Gobbo. Be God's sonties, 'twill be a hard way to hit; can you tell me whether one Launcelot, that dwells with him, dwell with him or no?

Launcelot. Talk you of young Master Launcelot? (*aside*) Mark me now, now will I raise the waters—Talk you of young Master Launcelot?

Gobbo. No master, sir, but a poor man's son; his father, though I say 't, is an honest exceeding poor man, and, God be thanked, well to live.

Launcelot. Well, let his father be what a' will, we talk of young Master Launcelot.

Gobbo. Your worship's friend, and Launcelot, sir.

Launcelot. But I pray you, ergo, old man, ergo,

I beseech you, talk you of young Master
Launcelot.

Gobbo. Of Launcelot, an 't please your master-
ship.

Launcelot. Ergo, Master Launcelot; talk not of
Master Launcelot, father, for the young gentleman, according to Fates and Destinies, and
such odd sayings, the Sisters Three, and such
branches of learning, is indeed deceased, or, as
you would say in plain terms, gone to heaven.

Gobbo. Marry, God forbid! the boy was the very
staff of my age, my very prop.

Launcelot. Do I look like a cudgel or a hovel-post,
a staff, or a prop? Do you know me, father?

Gobbo. Alack the day, I know you not, young gentleman, but, I pray you tell me, is my boy, God
rest his soul, alive or dead?

Launcelot. Do you not know me, father?

Gobbo. Alack, sir, I am sand-blind, I know you
not.

Launcelot. Nay, indeed, if you had your eyes you
might fail of the knowing me: it is a wise father
that knows his own child. Well, old man, I
will tell you news of your son, give me your
blessing, truth will come to light, murder cannot be hid long, a man's son may, but in the end
truth will out.

Gobbo. Pray you, sir, stand up, I am sure you
are not Launcelot my boy.

Launcelot. Pray you let's have no more fooling
about it, but give me your blessing: I am
Launcelot, your boy that was, your son that
is, your child that shall be.

Gobbo. I cannot think you are my son.

Launcelot. I know not what I shall think of that:
but I am Launcelot, the Jew's man, and I am
sure Margery your wife is my mother.

Gobbo. Her name is Margery, indeed; I'll be sworn, if thou be Launcelot, thou are mine own flesh and blood. Lord worshipp'd might he be, what a beard hast thou got! thou hast got more hair on thy chin than Dobbin my fill-horse has on his tail.

Launcelot. It should seem, then, that Dobbin's tail grows backward: I am sure he had more hair of his tail than I have of my face when I last saw him.

Gobbo. Lord, how art thou chang'd! How dost thou and thy master agree? I have brought him a present. How 'gree you now?

Launcelot. Well, well: but for mine own part, as I have set up my rest to run away, so I will not rest till I have run some ground. My master's a very Jew: give him a present! give him a halter: I am famish'd in his service; you may tell every finger I have with my ribs. Father, I am glad you are come; give me your present to one Master Bassanio, who indeed gives rare new liveries; if I serve not him, I will run as far as God has any ground. O rare fortune! here comes the man, to him, father, for I am a Jew if I serve the Jew any longer.

Enter Bassanio, with Leonardo and other followers

Bassanio. You may do so, but let it be so hasted that supper be ready at the farthest by five of the clock: see these letters delivered, put the liveries to making, and desire Gratiano to come anon to my lodging.   *Exit a Servant*

Launcelot. To him, father.

Gobbo. God bless your worship!

Bassanio. Gramercy! wouldst thou aught with me?

Gobbo. Here's my son, sir, a poor boy,—

Launcelot. Not a poor boy, sir, but the rich Jew's
man, that would, sir, as my father shall
specify,—

Gobbo. He hath a great infection, sir, as one
would say, to serve—

Launcelot. Indeed, the short and the long is, I
serve the Jew, and have a desire, as my father
shall specify,—

Gobbo. His master and he (saving your worship's
reverence,) are scarce cater-cousins,—

Launcelot. To be brief, the very truth is, that the
Jew having done me wrong, doth cause me,
as my father being I hope an old man shall
frutify unto you,—

Gobbo. I have here a dish of doves that I would
bestow upon your worship, and my suit is,—

Launcelot. In very brief, the suit is impertinent
to myself, as your worship shall know by this
honest old man, and, though I say it, though
old man, yet poor man, my father.

Bassanio. One speak for both, what would you?

Launcelot. Serve you, sir.

Gobbo. That is the very defect of the matter, sir.

Bassanio. I know thee well, thou hast obtain'd thy
suit;
Shylock thy master spoke with me this day,
And hath preferr'd thee, if it be preferment
To leave a rich Jew's service, to become
The follower of so poor a gentleman.

Launcelot. The old proverb is very well parted
between my master Shylock and you, sir; you
have the grace of God, sir, and he hath enough.

Bassanio. Thou speak'st it well; go, father, with
thy son.
Take leave of thy old master, and inquire
My lodging out; give him a livery
More guarded than his fellows': see it done.

Launcelot. Father, in. I cannot get a service, no, I have ne'er a tongue in my head. Well, if any man in Italy have a fairer table which doth offer to swear upon a book, I shall have good fortune. Go to, here's a simple line of life, here's a small trifle of wives, alas, fifteen wives is nothing, eleven widows and nine maids is a simple coming-in for one man, and then to 'scape drowning thrice, and to be in peril of my life with the edge of a feather-bed, here are simple scapes. Well, if Fortune be a woman, she's a good wench for this gear. Father come, I'll take my leave of the Jew in the twinkling.

> *Exeunt Launcelot and old Gobbo*

Bassanio. I pray thee, good Leonardo, think on this;

These things being bought and orderly bestow'd,

Return in haste, for I do feast to-night

My best-esteem'd acquaintance: hie thee, go.

Leonardo. My best endeavours shall be done herein.

Enter Gratiano

Gratiano. Where's your master?

Leonardo.   Yonder, sir, he walks.

> *Exit*

Gratiano. Signior Bassanio,—

Bassanio. Gratiano!

Gratiano. I have suit to you.

Bassanio.   You have obtain'd it.

Gratiano. You must not deny me, I must go with you to Belmont.

Bassanio. Why then, you must. But hear thee, Gratiano,

Thou art too wild, too rude, and bold of voice,

Parts that become thee happily enough,

And in such eyes as ours appear not faults
But where thou art not known; why there they
show
Something too liberal: pray thee take pain
To allay with some cold drops of modesty
Thy skipping spirit, lest through thy wild be-
haviour
I be misconster'd in the place I go to,
And lose my hopes.

Gratiano. Signior Bassanio, hear me;
If I do not put on a sober habit,
Talk with respect, and swear but now and
then,
Wear prayer-books in my pocket, look de-
murely,
Nay more, while grace is saying, hood mine
eyes
Thus with my hat, and sigh, and say 'amen,'
Use all the observance of civility,
Like one well studied in a sad ostent
To please his grandam, never trust me more.

Bassanio. Well, we shall see your bearing.

Gratiano. Nay, but I bar to-night, you shall not
gauge me
By what we do to-night.

Bassanio. No, that were pity:
I would entreat you rather to put on
Your boldest suit of mirth, for we have friends
That purpose merriment. But fare you well,
I have some business.

Gratiano. And I must to Lorenzo and the rest,
But we will visit you at supper-time.

Exeunt

SCENE III

The same. A room in Shylock's house

Enter Jessica and Launcelot

Jessica. I am sorry thou wilt leave my father so;
  Our house is hell, and thou, a merry devil,
  Didst rob it of some taste of tediousness.
  But fare thee well, there is a ducat for thee,
  And, Launcelot, soon at supper shalt thou see
  Lorenzo, who is thy new master's guest;
  Give him this letter, do it secretly,
  And so farewell: I would not have my father
  See me in talk with thee.
Launcelot. Adieu! tears exhibit my tongue. Most
  beautiful pagan, most sweet Jew! if a Christian
  do not play the knave, and get thee, I am much
  deceived. But adieu, these foolish drops do
  something drown my manly spirit: adieu.
Jessica. Farewell, good Launcelot.

                                     Exit Launcelot

  Alack, what heinous sin is it in me
  To be asham'd to be my father's child!
  But though I am a daughter to his blood,
  I am not to his manners. O Lorenzo,
  If thou keep promise I shall end this strife,
  Become a Christian and thy loving wife. *Exit*

SCENE IV

The same. A street

Enter Gratiano, Lorenzo, Salerio, and Solanio

Lorenzo. Nay, we will slink away in supper-time,
    Disguise us at my lodging, and return
    All in an hour.
Gratiano. We have not made good preparation.
Salerio. We have not spoke us yet of torch-
    bearers.
Solanio. 'Tis vile, unless it may be quaintly
    order'd,
    And better in my mind not undertook.
Lorenzo. 'Tis now but four o'clock; we have two
    hours
    To furnish us.

Enter Launcelot, with a letter

                Friend Launcelot, what's the news?
Launcelot. An it shall please you to break up this,
    it shall seem to signify.
Lorenzo. I know the hand, in faith, 'tis a fair
    hand,
    And whiter than the paper it writ on
    Is the fair hand that writ.
Gratiano.   Love-news, in faith.
Launcelot. By your leave, sir.
Lorenzo. Whither goest thou?
Launcelot. Marry, sir, to bid my old master the

Jew to sup to-night with my new master the
Christian.

Lorenzo. Hold, here, take this; tell gentle Jessica
I will not fail her; speak it privately.
Go, gentlemen,   *Exit Launcelot*
Will you prepare you for this masque to-night?
I am provided of a torch-bearer.

Salerio. Ay, marry, I'll be gone about it straight.

Solanio. And so will I.

Lorenzo.   Meet me and Gratiano
At Gratiano's lodging some hour hence.

Salerio. 'Tis good we do so.

                    Exeunt Salerio and Solanio

Gratiano. Was not that letter from fair Jessica?

Lorenzo. I must needs tell thee all. She hath
    directed
How I shall take her from her father's house,
What gold and jewels she is furnish'd with,
What page's suit she hath in readiness.
If e'er the Jew her father come to heaven,
It will be for his gentle daughter's sake,
And never dare misfortune cross her foot,
Unless she do it under this excuse,
That she is issue to a faithless Jew.
Come, go with me, peruse this as thou goest:
Fair Jessica shall be my torch-bearer.   *Exeunt*

SCENES V AND VI

The same. Before Shylock's house

Enter Shylock and Launcelot

Shylock. Well, thou shalt see, thy eyes shall be
   thy judge,
   The difference of old Shylock and Bassanio:—
   What, Jessica!—thou shalt not gormandise,
   As thou hast done with me:—What, Jessica!—
   And sleep, and snore, and rend apparel out;—
   Why, Jessica, I say!
Launcelot.   Why, Jessica!
Shylock. Who bids thee call? I do not bid thee
   call.
Launcelot. Your worship was wont to tell me I
   could do nothing without bidding.

Enter Jessica

Jessica. Call you? what is your will?
Shylock. I am bid forth to supper, Jessica;
   There are my keys. But wherefore should I go?
   I am not bid for love; they flatter me:
   But yet I'll go in hate, to feed upon
   The prodigal Christian. Jessica, my girl,
   Look to my house; I am right loath to go;
   There is some ill a-brewing towards my rest,
   For I did dream of money-bags to-night.
Launcelot. I beseech you, sir, go, my young mas-
   ter doth expect your reproach.
Shylock. So do I his.

Launcelot. And they have conspired together;
  I will not say you shall see a masque, but if you
  do, then it was not for nothing that my nose fell
  a-bleeding on Black-Monday last, at six o'clock
  i' the morning, falling out that year on Ash-
  Wednesday was four year, in the afternoon.

Shylock. What, are there masques? Hear you me,
  Jessica:
  Lock up my doors, and when you hear the
    drum
  And the vile squealing of the wry-neck'd fife,
  Clamber not you up to the casements then,
  Nor thrust your head into the public street
  To gaze on Christian fools with varnish'd faces;
  But stop my house's ears, I mean my casements,
  Let not the sound of shallow foppery enter
  My sober house. By Jacob's staff I swear
  I have no mind of feasting forth to-night:
  But I will go. Go you before me, sirrah,
  Say I will come.

Launcelot. I will go before, sir. Mistress, look out
  at window for all this;
        'There will come a Christian by,
           Will be worth a Jewess' eye.'   *Exit*

Shylock. What says that fool of Hagar's offspring,
  ha?

Jessica. His words were, 'Farewell, mistress,' nothing else.

Shylock. The patch is kind enough, but a huge
  feeder;
  Snail-slow in profit, and he sleeps by day
  More than the wild-cat: drones hive not with
    me,
  Therefore I part with him, and part with him
  To one that I would have him help to waste

His borrow'd purse. Well, Jessica, go in:
Perhaps I will return immediately.
Do as I bid you, shut doors after you:
Fast bind, fast find,
A proverb never stale in thrifty mind. *Exit*
Jessica. Farewell, and if my fortune be not crost,
I have a father, you a daughter, lost. *Exit*

Enter Gratiano and Salerio, masked

Gratiano. This is the pent-house under which Lorenzo
Desir'd us to make stand.
Salerio.   His hour is almost past.
Gratiano. And it is marvel he out-dwells his hour;
For lovers ever run before the clock.
Salerio. O, ten times faster Venus' pigeons fly
To seal love's bonds new-made, than they are wont
To keep obliged faith unforfeited!
Gratiano. That ever holds: who riseth from a feast
With that keen appetite that he sits down?
Where is the horse that doth untread again
His tedious measures with the unbated fire
That he did pace them first? All things that are
Are with more spirit chased than enjoy'd.
How like a younger or a prodigal
The scarfed bark puts from her native bay,
Hugg'd and embraced by the strumpet wind;
How like the prodigal doth she return,
With over-weather'd ribs and ragged sails,
Lean, rent, and beggar'd by the strumpet wind!
Salerio. Here comes Lorenzo, more of this here-after.

Enter Lorenzo

Lorenzo. Sweet friends, your patience for my
    long abode;
    Not I, but my affairs, have made you wait:
    When you shall please to play the thieves for
      wives,
    I'll watch as long for you then. Approach;
    Here dwells my father Jew. Ho! who's within?

Enter Jessica, above, in boy's clothes

Jessica. Who are you? Tell me, for more certainty,
    Albeit I'll swear that I do know your tongue.
Lorenzo. Lorenzo, and thy love.
Jessica. Lorenzo certain, and my love indeed,
    For who love I so much? And now who knows
    But you, Lorenzo, whether I am yours?
Lorenzo. Heaven and thy thoughts are witness
    that thou art.
Jessica. Here, catch this casket, it is worth the
    pains.
    I am glad 'tis night, you do not look on me,
    For I am much asham'd of my exchange:
    But love is blind, and lovers cannot see
    The pretty follies that themselves commit,
    For if they could, Cupid himself would blush
    To see me thus transformed to a boy.
Lorenzo. Descend, for you must be my torch-
    bearer.
Jessica. What, must I hold a candle to my shames?
    They in themselves, good sooth, are too too
    light.
    Why, 'tis an office of discovery, love,
    And I should be obscur'd.
Lorenzo.   So are you, sweet,
    Even in the lovely garnish of a boy.
    But come at once,

For the close night doth play the runaway,
And we are stay'd for at Bassanio's feast.

Jessica. I will make fast the doors and gild myself
With some moe ducats, and be with you
•straight. *Exit above*

Gratiano. Now, by my hood, a gentle, and no Jew.

Lorenzo. Beshrew me but I love her heartily,
For she is wise, if I can judge of her,
And fair she is, if that mine eyes be true,
And true she is, as she hath prov'd herself;
And therefore like herself, wise, fair, and true,
Shall she be placed in my constant soul.

Enter Jessica, below

What, art thou come? On, gentlemen, away!
Our masquing mates by this time for us stay.
Exit with Jessica and Salerio

Enter Antonio

Antonio. Who's there?

Gratiano. Signior Antonio?

Antonio. Fie, fie, Gratiano, where are all the rest?
'Tis nine o'clock, our friends all stay for you:
No masque to-night, the wind is come about,
Bassanio presently will go aboard:
I have sent twenty out to seek for you.

Gratiano. I am glad on 't; I desire no more de-
light
Than to be under sail, and gone to-night.
Exeunt

SCENE VII

Belmont. A room in Portia's house

Enter Portia, with the Prince of Morocco, and their trains

Portia. Go, draw aside the curtains, and discover
The several caskets to this noble prince.
Now make your choice.
Morocco. This first of gold, who this inscription
bears,
'Who chooseth me, shall gain what many men
desire;'
The second silver, which this promise carries,
'Who chooseth me, shall get as much as he
deserves;'
This third, dull lead, with warning all as blunt,
'Who chooseth me, must give and hazard all
he hath.'
How shall I know if I do choose the right?
Portia. The one of them contains my picture,
prince;
If you choose that, then I am yours withal.
Morocco. Some god direct my judgement! Let
me see;
I will survey the inscriptions, back again;
What says this leaden casket?
'Who chooseth me, must give an hazard all he
hath.'
Must give,—for what? for lead, hazard for lead?
This casket threatens; men that hazard all
Do it in hope of fair advantages:
A golden mind stoops not to shows of dross,
I'll then nor give nor hazard aught for lead.
What says the silver with her virgin hue?
'Who chooseth me, shall get as much as he de-
serves.'

As much as he deserves? Pause there, Morocco,
And weigh thy value with an even hand:
If thou be'st rated by thy estimation,
Thou dost deserve enough, and yet enough
May not extend so far as to the lady:
And yet to be afeard of my deserving
Were but a weak disabling of myself.
As much as I deserve? Why, that's the lady:
I do in birth deserve her, and in fortunes,
In graces, and in qualities of breeding;
But more than these, in love I do deserve;
What if I stray'd no further, but chose here?
Let's see once more this saying grav'd in gold;
'Who chooseth me, shall gain what many men
    desire.'
Why, that's the lady, all the world desires her;
From the four corners of the earth they come
To kiss this shrine, this mortal breathing saint:
The Hyrcanian deserts, and the vasty wilds
Of wide Arabia are as throughfares now
For princes to come view fair Portia:
The watery kingdom, whose ambitious head
Spits in the face of heaven, is no bar
To stop the foreign spirits, but they come
As o'er a brook to see fair Portia.
One of these three contains her heavenly pic-
    ture;
Is 't like that lead contains her? 'Twere damna-
    tion
To think so base a thought, it were too gross
To rib her cerecloth in the obscure grave;
Or shall I think in silver she's immur'd,
Being ten times undervalued to tried gold?
O sinful thought! Never so rich a gem
Was set in worse than gold. They have in Eng-
    land
A coin that bears the figure of an angel

Stamped in gold, but that's insculp'd upon;
But here an angel in a golden bed
Lies all within. Deliver me the key:
Here do I choose, and thrive I as I may!
Portia. There, take it, prince, and if my form lie
　　there,
　Then I am yours!
　　　　　　　　He unlocks the golden casket
Morocco.　　　O hell! what have we here?
　A carrion Death, within whose empty eye
　There is a written scroll! I'll read the writing.

(*reads*)　All that glisters is not gold,
　　　　　Often have you heard that told,
　　　　　Many a man his life hath sold
　　　　　But my outside to behold,
　　　　　Gilded tombs do worms infold:
　　　　　Had you been as wise as bold,
　　　　　Young in limbs, in judgement old,
　　　　　Your answer had not been inscroll'd,
　　　　　Fare you well, your suit is cold.

　Cold indeed, and labour lost,
　Then farewell heat, and welcome frost!
　Portia, adieu, I have too griev'd a heart
　To take a tedious leave: thus losers part.
　　　　Exit with his train. Flourish of cornets
Portia. A gentle riddance; draw the curtains, go.
　Let all of his complexion choose me so.
　　　　　　　　　　　　　　Exeunt

SCENE VIII

Venice. A street

Enter Salerio and Solanio

Salerio. Why, man, I saw Bassanio under sail,
  With him is Gratiano gone along;
  And in their ship I am sure Lorenzo is not.
Solanio. The villain Jew with outcries rais'd the
      Duke,
  Who went with him to search Bassanio's ship.
Salerio. He came too late, the ship was under sail,
  But there the Duke was given to understand
  That in a gondola were seen together
  Lorenzo and his amorous Jessica:
  Besides, Antonio certified the Duke
  They were not with Bassanio in his ship.
Solanio. I never heard a passion so confus'd,
  So strange, outrageous, and so variable,
  As the dog Jew did utter in the streets,
  'My daughter! O my ducats! O my daughter!
  Fled with a Christian! O my Christian ducats!
  Justice! the law! my ducats, and my daughter,
  A sealed bag, two sealed bags of ducats,
  Of double ducats, stolen from me by my
      daughter!
  And jewels, two stones, two rich and precious
      stones,
  Stolen by my daughter! Justice! find the girl!
  She hath the stones upon her, and the ducats!'

Salerio. Why, all the boys in Venice follow him,
    Crying his stones, his daughter, and his ducats.
Solanio. Let good Antonio look he keep his day,
    Or he shall pay for this.
Salerio.   Marry, well remember'd.
    I reason'd with a Frenchman yesterday,
    Who told me, in the narrow seas that part
    The French and English, there miscarried
    A vessel of our country richly fraught:
    I thought upon Antonio when he told me,
    And wish'd in silence that it were not his.
Solanio. You were best to tell Antonio what you
       hear,
    Yet do not suddenly, for it may grieve him.
Salerio. A kinder gentleman treads not the earth.
    I saw Bassanio and Antonio part:
    Bassanio told him he would make some speed
    Of his return: he answer'd, 'Do not so,
    Slubber not business for my sake, Bassanio,
    But stay the very riping of the time,
    And for the Jew's bond which he hath of me,
    Let it not enter in your mind of love:
    Be merry, and employ your chiefest thoughts
    To courtship, and such fair ostents of love
    As shall conveniently become you there;'
    And even there, his eye being big with tears,
    Turning his face, he put his hand behind him,
    And with affection wondrous sensible
    He wrung Bassanio's hand, and so they parted.
Solanio. I think he only loves the world for him.
    I pray thee let us go and find him out,
    And quicken his embraced heaviness
    With some delight or other.
Salerio.   Do we so. *Exeunt*

SCENE IX

Belmont. A room in Portia's house

Enter Nerissa and a Servitor

Nerissa. Quick, quick, I pray thee, draw the cur-
   tain straight;
   The Prince of Arragon hath ta'en his oath,
   And comes to his election presently.

   *Flourish of cornets. Enter the Prince of Arragon,
   Portia, and their trains*

Portia. Behold, there stand the caskets, noble
   prince;
   If you choose that wherein I am contain'd,
   Straight shall our nuptial rites be solemniz'd:
   But if you fail, without more speech, my lord,
   You must be gone from hence immediately.
Arragon. I am enjoin'd by oath to observe three
   things:
   First, never to unfold to any one
   Which casket 'twas I chose; next, if I fail
   Of the right casket, never in my life
   To woo a maid in way of marriage: lastly,
   If I do fail in fortune of my choice,
   Immediately to leave you, and be gone.
Portia. To these injunctions every one doth swear
   That comes to hazard for my worthless self.
Arragon. And so have I address'd me; fortune now
   To my heart's hope! Gold, silver, and base lead.
   'Who chooseth me, must give and hazard all
   he hath.'

You shall look fairer ere I give or hazard.
What says the golden chest? ha! let me see:
'Who chooseth me, shall gain what many men
    desire.'
What many men desire? that 'many' may be
    meant
By the fool multitude, that choose by show,
Not learning more than the fond eye doth
    teach,
Which pries not to the interior, but, like the
    martlet,
Builds in the weather on the outward wall,
Even in the force and road of casualty.
I will not choose what many men desire,
Because I will not jump with common spirits,
And rank me with the barbarous multitudes.
Why then, to thee, thou silver treasure-house,
Tell me once more what title thou dost bear;
'Who chooseth me shall get as much as he
    deserves:'
And well said too; for who shall go about
To cozen fortune, and be honourable
Without the stamp of merit? Let none presume
To wear an undeserved dignity.
O, that estates, degrees, and offices
Were not deriv'd corruptly, and that clear
    honour
Were purchas'd by the merit of the wearer!
How many then should cover that stand bare!
How many be commanded that command!
How much low peasantry would then be
    glean'd
From the true seed of honour! and how much
    honour
Pick'd from the chaff and ruin of the times,

To be new-varnish'd! Well, but to my choice:
'Who chooseth me shall get as much as he de-
    serves;'
I will assume desert; give me a key for this,
And instantly unlock my fortunes here.
> *He opens the silver casket*
Portia. *(aside)* Too long a pause for that which
    you find there.
Arragon. What's here? the portrait of a blinking
    idiot,
Presenting me a schedule! I will read it.
How much unlike art thou to Portia!
How much unlike my hopes and my deserv-
    ings!
'Who chooseth me, shall have as much as he
    deserves?'
Did I deserve no more than a fool's head?
Is that my prize? are my deserts no better?
Portia. To offend, and judge, are distinct offices,
    And of opposed natures.
Arragon.   What is here?

(*reads*) The fire seven times tried this,
            Seven times tried that judgement is,
            That did never choose amiss.
            Some there be that shadows kiss,
            Such have but a shadow's bliss:
            There be fools alive, I wis,
            Silver'd o'er, and so was this.
            Take what wife you will to bed,
            I will ever be your head:
            So be gone, you are sped.

            Still more fool I shall appear
            By the time I linger here:
            With one fool's head I came to woo,
            But I go away with two.

Sweet, adieu; I'll keep my oath,
Patiently to bear my wroth.

Exeunt Arragon and train

Portia   Thus hath the candle sing'd the moth.
O, these deliberate fools! when they do choose,
They have the wisdom by their wit to lose.
Nerissa. The ancient saying is no heresy,
Hanging and wiving goes by destiny.
Portia. Come, draw the curtain, Nerissa.

Enter a Servant

Servant. Where is my lady?
Portia.   Here: what would my lord?
Servant. Madam, there is alighted at your gate
A young Venetian, one that comes before
To signify the approaching of his lord,
From whom he bringeth sensible regrets;
To wit (besides commends and courteous
    breath)
Gifts of rich value; yet I have not seen
So likely an ambassador of love.
A day in April never came so sweet
To show how costly summer was at hand,
As this fore-spurrer comes before his lord.
Portia. No more, I pray thee; I am half afeard
Thou wilt say anon he is some kin to thee,
Thou spend'st such high-day wit in praising
    him:
Come, come, Nerissa, for I long to see
Quick Cupid's post that comes so mannerly.
Nerissa. Bassanio, lord Love, if thy will it be!

Exeunt

ACT III

SCENE I

Venice. A street

Enter Solanio and Salerio

Solanio. Now, what news on the Rialto?

Salerio. Why, yet it lives there uncheck'd, that Antonio hath a ship of rich lading wreck'd on the narrow seas; the Goodwins I think they call the place, a very dangerous flat, and fatal, where the carcases of many a tall ship lie buried, as they say, if my gossip Report be an honest woman of her word.

Solanio. I would she were as lying a gossip in that as ever knapp'd ginger, or made her neighbours believe she wept for the death of a third husband: but it is true, without any slips of prolixity, or crossing the plain highway of talk, that the good Antonio, the honest Antonio,— O that I had a title good enough to keep his name company!—

Salerio. Come, the full stop.

Solanio. Ha! what sayest thou? Why, the end is, he hath lost a ship.

Salerio. I would it might prove the end of his losses.

Solanio. Let me say 'amen' betimes, lest the devil cross my prayer, for here he comes in the likeness of a Jew.

Enter Shylock

How now, Shylock, what news among the merchants?

Shylock. You knew, none so well, none so well
as you, of my daughter's flight.

Salerio. That's certain; I, for my part, knew the
tailor that made the wings she flew withal.

Solanio. And Shylock, for his own part, knew the
bird was fledg'd; and then it is the complexion
of them all to leave the dam.

Shylock. She is damn'd for it.

Salerio. That's certain, if the devil may be her
judge.

Shylock. My own flesh and blood to rebel!

Solanio. Out upon it, old carrion! rebels it at these
years?

Shylock. I say my daughter is my flesh and blood.

Salerio. There is more difference between thy
flesh and hers, than between jet and ivory,
more between your bloods, than there is between red wine and rhenish. But tell us, do
you hear whether Antonio have had any loss
at sea or no?

Shylock. There I have another bad match, a bankrupt, a prodigal, who dare scarce show his head
on the Rialto, a beggar, that was used to come
so smug upon the mart; let him look to his bond,
he was wont to call me usurer, let him look to
his bond, he was wont to lend money for a
Christian curtsy, let him look to his bond.

Salerio. Why, I am sure, if he forfeit, thou wilt
not take his flesh; what's that good for?

Shylock. To bait fish withal, if it will feed nothing
else, it will feed my revenge. He hath disgrac'd
me, and hinder'd me half a million, laugh'd at

my losses, mock'd at my gains, scorned my nation, thwarted my bargains, cool'd my friends,
heated mine enemies, and what's his reason? I
am a Jew. Hath not a Jew eyes, hath not a Jew
hands, organs, dimensions, senses, affections,
passions, fed with the same food, hurt with the
same weapons, subject to the same diseases,
healed by the same means, warmed and cooled
by the same winter and summer as a Christian
is? If you prick us, do we not bleed? if you
tickle us do we not laugh, if you poison us do
we not die, and if you wrong us, shall we not
revenge? if we are like you in the rest, we will
resemble you in that. If a Jew wrong a Christian, what is his humility? Revenge. If a Christian wrong a Jew, what should his sufferance
be by Christian example? Why, revenge. The
villany you teach me I will execute, and it shall
go hard but I will better the instruction.

Enter a Servant

Servant. Gentlemen, my master Antonio is at his
house, and desires to speak with you both.
Salerio. We have been up and down to seek him.

Enter Tubal

Solanio. Here comes another of the tribe; a third
cannot be match'd, unless the devil himself
turn Jew.

    Exeunt Solanio, Salerio, and Servant
Shylock. How now, Tubal, what news from
Genoa? hast thou found my daughter?
Tubal. I often came where I did hear of her, but
cannot find her.
Shylock. Why, there, there, there, there! a dia-
mond gone, cost me two thousand ducats in

Frankfort! The curse never fell upon our nation till now, I never felt it till now, two thousand ducats in that, and other precious, precious jewels. I would my daughter were dead at my foot, and the jewels in her ear! would she were hears'd at my foot, and the ducats in her coffin! No news of them? Why, so:—and I know not what's spent in the search: why, thou loss upon loss! the thief gone with so much, and so much to find the thief, and no satisfaction, no revenge, nor no ill luck stirring but what lights o' my shoulders, no sighs but o' my breathing, no tears but o' my shedding.

Tubal. Yes, other men have ill luck too; Antonio, as I heard in Genoa,—

Shylock. What, what, what? ill luck, ill luck?

Tubal. Hath an argosy cast away, coming from Tripolis.

Shylock. I thank God, I thank God! Is it true, is it true?

Tubal. I spoke with some of the sailors that escaped the wreck.

Shylock. I thank thee, good Tubal: good news, good news! ha, ha! here in Genoa.

Tubal. Your daughter spent in Genoa, as I heard, one night fourscore ducats.

Shylock. Thou stick'st a dagger in me, I shall never see my gold again: fourscore ducats at a sitting! fourscore ducats!

Tubal. There came divers of Antonio's creditors in my company to Venice, that swear he cannot choose but break.

Shylock. I am very glad of it, I'll plague him, I'll torture him, I am glad of it.

Tubal. One of them showed me a ring that he had of your daughter for a monkey.

Shylock. Out upon her! Thou torturest me, Tubal, it was my turquoise, I had it of Leah when I was a bachelor: I would not have given it for a wilderness of monkeys.

Tubal. But Antonio is certainly undone.

Shylock. Nay, that's true, that's very true. Go, Tubal, fee me an officer, bespeak him a fortnight before, I will have the heart of him if he forfeit, for were he out of Venice I can make what merchandise I will. Go, Tubal, and meet me at our synagogue; go, good Tubal, at our synagogue, Tubal.   *Exeunt*

SCENE II

Belmont. A room in Portia's house

Enter Bassanio, Portia, Gratiano, Nerissa, and Attendants

Portia. I pray you tarry, pause a day or two
  Before you hazard, for, in choosing wrong,
  I lose your company; therefore forbear awhile.
  There's something tells me (but it is not love)
  I would not lose you, and you know yourself,
  Hate counsels not in such a quality.
  But lest you should not understand me well,—
  And yet a maiden hath no tongue, but
    thought,—
  I would detain you here some month or two
  Before you venture for me. I could teach you
  How to choose right, but then I am forsworn;
  So will I never be, so may you miss me,
  But if you do, you'll make me wish a sin,
  That I had been forsworn. Beshrew your eyes,
  They have o'er-look'd me and divided me,
  One half of me is yours, the other half yours,
  Mine own, I would say; but if mine, then yours,
  And so all yours! O, these naughty times
  Puts bars between the owners and their rights,
  And so, though yours, not yours. Prove it so,
  Let fortune go to hell for it, not I.
  I speak too long, but 'tis to peize the time,
  To eke it, and to draw it out in length,
  To stay you from election.
Bassanio.   Let me choose,
  For as I am, I live upon the rack.
Portia. Upon the rack, Bassanio? then confess
  What treason there is mingled with your love.

Bassanio. None but that ugly treason of mistrust,
  Which makes me fear the enjoying of my love:
  There may as well be amity and life
  'Tween snow and fire, as treason and my love.
Portia. Ay, but I fear you speak upon the rack,
  Where men enforced do speak any thing.
Bassanio. Promise me life, and I'll confess the
    truth.
Portia. Well then, confess and live.
Bassanio.   'Confess,' and 'love,'
  Had been the very sum of my confession:
  O happy torment, when my torturer
  Doth teach me answers for deliverance!
  But let me to my fortune and the caskets.
Portia. Away, then! I am lock'd in one of them:
  If you do love me, you will find me out.
  Nerissa and the rest, stand all aloof,
  Let music sound while he doth make his
    choice,
  Then, if he lose, he makes a swan-like end,
  Fading in music: that the comparison
  May stand more proper, my eye shall be the
    stream
  And watery death-bed for him. He may win,
  And what is music then? Then music is
  Even as the flourish, when true subjects bow
  To a new-crowned monarch: such it is,
  As are those dulcet sounds in break of day,
  That creep into the dreaming bridegroom's
    ear,
  And summon him to marriage. Now he goes
  With no less presence, but with much more
    love,
  Than young Alcides, when he did redeem
  The virgin tribute, paid by howling Troy
  To the sea-monster: I stand for sacrifice;

The rest aloof are the Dardanian wives,
With bleared visages come forth to view
The issue of th' exploit. Go, Hercules!
Live thou, I live: with much much more
    dismay
I view the fight than thou that mak'st the fray.

A song, the whilst Bassanio comments on the caskets
to himself

Tell me where is fancy bred,
Or in the heart or in the head,
How begot, how nourished?
    Reply, reply.
It is engender'd in the eyes,
With gazing fed, and fancy dies
In the cradle where it lies.
    Let us all ring fancy's knell;
    I'll begin it,—Ding, dong, bell.

All.   Ding, dong, bell.
Bassanio. So may the outward shows be least
    themselves:
The world is still deceiv'd with ornament;
In law, what plea so tainted and corrupt,
But, being season'd with a gracious voice,
Obscures the show of evil? In religion,
What damned error, but some sober brow
Will bless it, and approve it with a text,
Hiding the grossness with fair ornament?
There is no vice so simple, but assumes
Some mark of virtue on his outward parts:
How many cowards whose hearts are all as
    false
As stairs of sand wear yet upon their chins
The beards of Hercules and frowning Mars,
Who, inward search'd, have livers white as
    milk,

And these assume but valour's excrement
To render them redoubted! Look on beauty,
And you shall see 'tis purchas'd by the weight,
Which therein works a miracle in nature,
Making them lightest that wear most of it:
So are those crisped snaky golden locks
Which make such wanton gambols with the
    wind
Upon supposed fairness, often known
To be the dowry of a second head,
The skull that bred them in the sepulchre.
Thus ornament is but the guiled shore
To a most dangerous sea; the beauteous scarf
Veiling an Indian; beauty, in a word,
The seeming truth which cunning times put
    on
To entrap the wisest. Therefore, thou gaudy
    gold,
Hard food for Midas, I will none of thee,
Nor none of thee, thou pale and common
    drudge
'Tween man and man: but thou, thou meagre
    lead,
Which rather threaten'st than dost promise
    aught,
Thy plainness moves me more than eloquence,
And here choose I, joy be the consequence!
Portia. (*aside*) How all the other passions fleet to
    air,
As doubtful thoughts, and rash-embrac'd
    despair,
And shudd'ring fear, and green-eyed jealousy!
O love, be moderate, allay thy ecstasy,
In measure rain thy joy, scant this excess!
I feel too much thy blessing, make it less,
For fear I surfeit!

Bassanio.   What find I here?
                    Opening the leaden casket
Fair Portia's counterfeit! What demi-god
Hath come so near creation? Move these eyes?
Or whether, riding on the balls of mine,
Seem they in motion? Here are sever'd lips
Parted with sugar breath; so sweet a bar
Should sunder such sweet friends. Here in her
    hairs
The painter plays the spider, and hath woven
A golden mesh to entrap the hearts of men
Faster than gnats in cobwebs; but her eyes,—
How could he see to do them? having made
    one,
Methinks it should have power to steal both his
And leave itself unfurnish'd. Yet look how far
The substance of my praise doth wrong this
    shadow
In underprizing it, so far this shadow
Doth limp behind the substance. Here's the
    scroll,
The continent and summary of my fortune.

(reads)
            You that choose not by the view,
            Chance as fair, and choose as true!
            Since this fortune falls to you,
            Be content, and seek no new.
            If you be well pleas'd with this,
            And hold your fortune for your bliss,
            Turn you where your lady is,
            And claim her with a loving kiss.

    A gentle scroll. Fair lady, by your leave,
    I come by note to give, and to receive,
    Like one of two contending in a prize,
    That thinks he hath done well in people's eyes;

Hearing applause and universal shout,
Giddy in spirit, still gazing in a doubt
Whether those peals of praise be his or no,
So, thrice-fair lady, stand I, even so,
As doubtful whether what I see be true,
Until confirm'd, sign'd, ratified by you.

Portia. You see me, Lord Bassanio, where I stand,
Such as I am; though for myself alone
I would not be ambitious in my wish
To wish myself much better, yet for you,
I would be trebled twenty times myself,
A thousand times more fair, ten thousand times
More rich;
That only to stand high in your account,
I might in virtues, beauties, livings, friends,
Exceed account; but the full sum of me
Is sum of something; which, to term in gross,
Is an unlesson'd girl, unschool'd, unpractis'd,
Happy in this, she is not yet so old
But she may learn; happier than this,
She is not bred so dull but she can learn;
Happiest of all, is that her gentle spirit
Commits itself to yours to be directed,
As from her lord, her governor, her king.
Myself, and what is mine, to you and yours
Is now converted: but now I was the lord
Of this fair mansion, master of my servants,
Queen o'er myself; and even now, but now,
This house, these servants, and this same my-
    self,
Are yours, my lord's: I give them with this ring,
Which when you part from, lose, or give away,
Let it presage the ruin of your love,
And be my vantage to exclaim on you.

Bassanio. Madam, you have bereft me of all
    words,
Only my blood speaks to you in my veins,

And there is such confusion in my powers,
As, after some oration fairly spoke
By a beloved prince, there doth appear
Among the buzzing pleased multitude;
Where every something, being blent together,
Turns to a wild of nothing, save of joy,
Express'd, and not express'd. But when this ring
Parts from this finger, then parts life from hence,
O, then be bold to say Bassanio's dead!

Nerissa. My lord and lady, it is now our time,
That have stood by and seen our wishes
prosper,
To cry 'good joy, good joy, my lord and lady!'

Gratiano. My lord Bassanio, and my gentle lady,
I wish you all the joy that you can wish;
For I am sure you can wish none from me:
And when your honours mean to solemnize
The bargain of your faith, I do beseech you,
Even at that time I may be married too.

Bassanio. With all my heart, so thou canst get a
wife.

Gratiano. I thank your lordship, you have got me
one.
My eyes, my lord, can look as swift as yours:
You saw the mistress, I beheld the maid;
You lov'd, I lov'd for intermission;
No more pertains to me, my lord, than you.
Your fortune stood upon the caskets there,
And so did mine too, as the matter falls;
For wooing here until I sweat again,
And swearing till my very roof was dry
With oaths of love, at last, if promise last,
I got a promise of this fair one here
To have her love; provided that your fortune
Achiev'd her mistress.

Portia. Is this true, Nerissa?

Nerissa. Madam, it is, so you stand pleas'd withal.

Bassanio. And do you, Gratiano, mean good faith?

Gratiano. Yes, faith, my lord.

Bassanio. Our feast shall be much honoured in
your marriage.

Gratiano. We'll play with them the first boy for a
thousand ducats.

Nerissa. What, and stake down?

Gratiano. No, we shall ne'er win at that sport, and
stake down.

But who comes here? Lorenzo and his infidel?
What, and my old Venetian friend Salerio?

*Enter Lorenzo, Jessica, and Salerio,
a Messenger from Venice*

Bassanio. Lorenzo and Salerio, welcome hither,
If that the youth of my new interest here
Have power to bid you welcome. By your leave,
I bid my very friends and countrymen,
Sweet Portia, welcome.

Portia. So do I, my lord,
They are entirely welcome.

Lorenzo. I thank your honour; for my part, my
lord,
My purpose was not to have seen you here,
But meeting with Salerio by the way,
He did entreat me, past all saying nay,
To come with him along.

Salerio. I did, my lord,
And I have reason for it; Signior Antonio
Commends him to you.

Gives Bassanio a letter

Bassanio. Ere I ope his letter,
I pray you tell me how my good friend doth.

Salerio. Not sick, my lord, unless it be in mind,

Nor well, unless in mind: his letter there
Will show you his estate.

Bassanio opens the letter

Gratiano. Nerissa, cheer yon stranger, bid her
    welcome.
    Your hand, Salerio, what's the news from
        Venice?
    How doth that royal merchant, good Antonio?
    I know he will be glad of our success,
    We are the Jasons, we have won the fleece.
Salerio. I would you had won the fleece that he
    hath lost.
Portia. There are some shrewd contents in yon
    same paper,
    That steals the colour from Bassanio s cheek,
    Some dear friend dead, else nothing in the
        world
    Could turn so much the constitution
    Of any constant man. What, worse and worse?
    With leave, Bassanio, I am half yourself,
    And I must freely have the half of anything
    That this same paper brings you.
Bassanio.   O sweet Portia,
    Here are a few of the unpleasant'st words
    That ever blotted paper! Gentle lady,
    When I did first impart my love to you,
    I freely told you all the wealth I had
    Ran in my veins, I was a gentleman,
    And then I told you true: and yet, dear lady,
    Rating myself at nothing, you shall see
    How much I was a braggart; when I told you
    My state was nothing, I should then have told
        you
    That I was worse than nothing; for, indeed,
    I have engag'd myself to a dear friend,
    Engag'd my friend to his mere enemy,

To feed my means. Here is a letter, lady,
The paper as the body of my friend,
And every word in it a gaping wound
Issuing life-blood. But is it true, Salerio?
Hath all his ventures fail'd? What, not one hit?
From Tripolis, from Mexico, and England,
From Lisbon, Barbary, and India,
And not one vessel scape the dreadful touch
Of merchant-marring rocks?
Salerio.   Not one, my lord.
Besides, it should appear, that if he had
The present money to discharge the Jew,
He would not take it: never did I know
A creature that did bear the shape of man
So keen and greedy to confound a man.
He plies the Duke at morning and at night,
And doth impeach the freedom of the state
If they deny him justice: twenty merchants,
The Duke himself, and the magnificoes
Of greatest port, have all persuaded with him,
But none can drive him from the envious plea
Of forfeiture, of justice, and his bond.
Jessica. When I was with him, I have heard him
     swear
To Tubal and to Chus, his countrymen,
That he would rather have Antonio's flesh
Than twenty times the value of the sum
That he did owe him: and I know, my lord,
If law, authority, and power deny not,
It will go hard with poor Antonio.
Portia. Is it your dear friend that is thus in
     trouble?
Bassanio. The dearest friend to me, the kindest
     man,
The best-condition'd and unwearied spirit
In doing courtesies; and one in whom

The ancient Roman honour more appears
Than any that draws breath in Italy.
Portia. What sum owes he the Jew?
Bassanio. For me three thousand ducats.
Portia.   What, no more?
　Pay him six thousand, and deface the bond;
　Double six thousand, and then treble that,
　Before a friend of this description
　Shall lose a hair thorough Bassanio's fault.
　First go with me to church, and call me wife,
　And then away to Venice to your friend;
　For never shall you lie by Portia's side
　With an unquiet soul. You shall have gold
　To pay the petty debt twenty times over.
　When it is paid, bring your true friend along;
　My maid Nerissa and myself meantime
　Will live as maids and widows. Come, away,
　For you shall hence upon your wedding-day:
　Bid your friends welcome, show a merry cheer,
　Since you are dear bought, I will love you dear.
　But let me hear the letter of your friend.
Bassanio. (*reads*) Sweet Bassanio, my ships have
　all miscarried, my creditors grow cruel, my es-
　tate is very low, my bond to the Jew is forfeit,
　and since in paying it, it is impossible I should
　live, all debts are clear'd between you and I, if
　I might but see you at my death: notwithstand-
　ing, use your pleasure; if your love do not per-
　suade you to come, let not my letter.
Portia. O love, dispatch all business, and be gone!
Bassanio. Since I have your good leave to go
　　　away,
　　I will make haste: but, till I come again,
　No bed shall e'er be guilty of my stay.
　　Nor rest be interposer 'twixt us twain.
　　　　　　　　　　　　　　　　Exeunt

SCENE III

Enter Shylock, Solanio, Antonio, and Gaoler

Shylock. Gaoler, look to him, tell not me of mercy;
    This is the fool that lent out money gratis:
    Gaoler, look to him.
Antonio.   Hear me yet, good Shylock.
Shylock. I'll have my bond, speak not against my
        bond,
    I have sworn an oath, that I will have my bond:
    Thou call'dst me dog before thou hadst a cause,
    But, since I am a dog, beware my fangs;
    The Duke shall grant me justice, I do wonder,
    Thou naughty gaoler, that thou art so fond
    To come abroad with him at his request.
Antonio. I pray thee hear me speak.
Shylock. I'll have my bond. I will not hear thee
        speak,
    I'll have my bond, and therefore speak no more.
    I'll not be made a soft and dull-eyed fool,
    To shake the head, relent, and sigh, and yield
    To Christian intercessors. Follow not,
    I'll have no speaking, I will have my bond.
                         Exit
Solanio. It is the most impenetrable cur
    That ever kept with men.
Antonio.   Let him alone,
    I'll follow him no more with bootless prayers.

He seeks my life, his reason well I know:
I oft deliver'd from his forfeitures
Many that have at times made moan to me,
Therefore he hates me.

Solanio.   I am sure the Duke
Will never grant this forfeiture to hold.

Antonio. The Duke cannot deny the course of
    law:
For the commodity that strangers have
With us in Venice, if it be denied,
Will much impeach the justice of the state,
Since that the trade and profit of the city
Consisteth of all nations. Therefore, go;
These griefs and losses have so bated me
That I shall hardly spare a pound of flesh
To-morrow, to my bloody creditor.
Well, gaoler, on; pray God Bassanio come
To see me pay his debt, and then I care not!

                                        Exeunt

SCENE IV

Belmont. A room in Portia's house

Enter Portia, Nerissa, Lorenzo, Jessica, and Balthasar

Lorenzo. Madam, although I speak it in your
    presence,
  You have a noble and a true conceit
  Of god-like amity, which appears most strongly
  In bearing thus the absence of your lord.
  But if you knew to whom you show this
    honour,
  How true a gentleman you send relief,
  How dear a lover of my lord your husband,
  I know you would be prouder of the work
  Than customary bounty can enforce you.
Portia. I never did repent for doing good,
  Nor shall not now: for in companions
  That do converse and waste the time together,
  Whose souls do bear an equal yoke of love,
  There must be needs a like proportion
  Of lineaments, of manners, and of spirit;
  Which makes me think that this Antonio,
  Being the bosom lover of my lord,
  Must needs be like my lord. If it be so,
  How little is the cost I have bestow'd
  In purchasing the semblance of my soul
  From out the state of hellish cruelty!
  This comes too near the praising of myself,
  Therefore no more of it: hear other things.

Lorenzo, I commit into your hands
The husbandry and manage of my house,
Until my lord's return: for mine own part,
I have toward heaven breath'd a secret vow,
To live in prayer and contemplation,
Only attended by Nerissa here,
Until her husband and my lord's return:
There is a monastery two miles off,
And there we will abide. I do desire you
Not to deny this imposition,
The which my love and some necessity
Now lays upon you.

Lorenzo.   Madam, with all my heart,
I shall obey you in all fair commands.

Portia. My people do already know my mind,
And will acknowledge you and Jessica
In place of Lord Bassanio and myself.
So fare you well till we shall meet again.

Lorenzo. Fair thoughts and happy hours attend
        on you!

Jessica. I wish your ladyship all heart's content.

Portia. I thank you for your wish, and am well
        pleas'd
To wish it back on you: fare you well, Jessica.

                        Exeunt Jessica and Lorenzo

Now, Balthasar,
As I have ever found thee honest-true,
So let me find thee still: take this same letter,
And use thou all the endeavour of a man,
In speed to Padua, see thou render this
Into my cousin's hand, Doctor Bellario,
And look what notes and garments he doth give
        thee,
Bring them, I pray thee, with imagin'd speed
Unto the tranect, to the common ferry
Which trades to Venice; waste no time in
        words,

But get thee gone, I shall be there before thee.
Balthasar. Madam, I go with all convenient
speed.   *Exit*
Portia. Come on, Nerissa, I have work in hand
That you yet know not of; we'll see our
husbands
Before they think of us.
Nerissa.   Shall they see us?
Portia. They shall, Nerissa; but in such a habit,
That they shall think we are accomplished
With that we lack; I'll hold thee any wager,
When we are both accoutred like young men,
I'll prove the prettier fellow of the two,
And wear my dagger with the braver grace,
And speak between the change of man and
boy,
With a reed voice, and turn two mincing steps
Into a manly stride; and speak of frays
Like a fine bragging youth; and tell quaint lies
How honourable ladies sought my love,
Which I denying, they fell sick and died;
I could not do withal: then I'll repent,
And wish, for all that, that I had not kill'd
them;
And twenty of these puny lies I'll tell,
That men shall swear I have discontinued
school
Above a twelvemonth: I have within my mind
A thousand raw tricks of these bragging Jacks,
Which I will practise.
Nerissa.   Why, shall we turn to men?
Portia. Fie, what a question 's that,
If thou wert near a lewd interpreter!
But come, I'll tell thee all my whole device
When I am in my coach, which stays for us
At the park-gate; and therefore haste away,
For we must measure twenty miles to-day.
                                                    Exeunt

87

SCENE V

The same. A garden

Enter Launcelot and Jessica

Launcelot. Yes truly, for look you, the sins of the
father are to be laid upon the children, therefore, I promise you, I fear you. I was always
plain with you, and so now I speak my agitation
of the matter: therefore be o' good cheer, for
truly I think you are damn'd, there is but one
hope in it that can do you any good, and that
is but a kind of bastard hope neither.

Jessica. And what hope is that, I pray thee?

Launcelot. Marry, you may partly hope that your
father got you not, that you are not the Jew's
daughter.

Jessica. That were a kind of bastard hope indeed,
so the sins of my mother should be visited upon
me.

Launcelot. Truly then I fear you are damn'd both
by father and mother: thus when I shun Scylla
your father, I fall into Charybdis your mother;
well, you are gone both ways.

Jessica. I shall be sav'd by my husband, he hath
made me a Christian.

Launcelot. Truly the more to blame he, we were
Christians enow before, e'en as many as could
well live one by another: this making of Christians will raise the price of hogs, if we grow all
to be pork-eaters, we shall not shortly have a
rasher on the coals for money.

Enter Lorenzo

Jessica. I'll tell my husband, Launcelot, what you
say; here he comes.

Lorenzo. I shall grow jealous of you shortly, Launcelot, if you thus get my wife into corners!

Jessica. Nay, you need not fear us, Lorenzo, Launcelot and I are out; he tells me flatly there's no mercy for me in heaven, because I am a Jew's daughter: and he says you are no good member of the commonwealth, for in converting Jews to Christians, you raise the price of pork.

Lorenzo. I shall answer that better to the commonwealth than you can the getting up of the negro's belly: the Moor is with child by you, Launcelot.

Launcelot. It is much that the Moor should be more than reason: but if she be less than an honest woman, she is indeed more than I took her for.

Lorenzo. How every fool can play upon the word! I think the best grace of wit will shortly turn into silence, and discourse grow commendable in none only but parrots. Go in, sirrah, bid them prepare for dinner.

Launcelot. That is done, sir; they have all stomachs.

Lorenzo. Goodly Lord, what a wit-snapper are you! then bid them prepare dinner.

Launcelot. That is done too, sir, only 'cover' is the word.

Lorenzo. Will you cover, then, sir?

Launcelot. Not so, sir, neither; I know my duty.

Lorenzo. Yet more quarrelling with occasion! Wilt thou show the whole wealth of thy wit in an instant? I pray thee understand a plain man in his plain meaning: go to thy fellows, bid them cover the table, serve in the meat, and we will come in to dinner.

Launcelot. For the table, sir, it shall be serv'd in, for the meat, sir, it shall be cover'd, for your coming in to dinner, sir, why, let it be as humours and conceits shall govern. *Exit*
Lorenzo. O dear discretion, how his words are suited!
The fool hath planted in his memory
An army of good words, and I do know
A many fools, that stand in better place,
Garnish'd like him, that for a tricksy word
Defy the matter. How cheer'st thou, Jessica?
And now, good sweet, say thy opinion,
How dost thou like the Lord Bassanio's wife?
Jessica. Past all expressing. It is very meet
The Lord Bassanio live an upright life,
For, having such a blessing in his lady,
He finds the joys of heaven here on earth,
And if on earth he do not merit it,
In reason he should never come to heaven.
Why, if two gods should play some heavenly match,
And on the wager lay two earthly women,
And Portia one, there must be something else
Pawn'd with the other; for the poor rude world
Hath not her fellow.
Lorenzo. Even such a husband
Hast thou of me as she is for a wife.
Jessica. Nay, but ask my opinion too of that.
Lorenzo. I will anon; first let us go to dinner.
Jessica. Nay, let me praise you while I have a stomach.
Lorenzo. No, pray thee, let it serve for table-talk,
Then, howsoe'er thou speak'st, 'mong other things
I shall digest it.
Jessica. Well, I'll set you forth. *Exeunt*

ACT IV

SCENE I

Venice. A court of justice

*Enter the Duke, the Magnificoes, Antonio, Bassanio,
Gratiano, Salerio, and others*

Duke. What, is Antonio here?

Antonio. Ready, so please your Grace.

Duke. I am sorry for thee, thou art come to answer
A stony adversary, an inhuman wretch,
Uncapable of pity, void and empty
From any dram of mercy.

Antonio.   I have heard
Your Grace hath ta'en great pains to qualify
His rigorous course; but since he stands obdurate,
And that no lawful means can carry me
Out of his envy's reach, I do oppose
My patience to his fury, and am arm'd
To suffer with a quietness of spirit,
The very tyranny and rage of his.

Duke. Go one and call the Jew into the court.

Salerio. He is ready at the door: he comes, my lord.

Enter Shylock

Duke. Make room, and let him stand before our face.
Shylock, the world thinks, and I think so too,
That thou but lead'st this fashion of thy malice

To the last hour of act, and then 'tis thought
Thou'lt show thy mercy and remorse more
strange
Than is thy strange apparent cruelty;
And where thou now exacts the penalty,
Which is a pound of this poor merchant's flesh,
Thou wilt not only loose the forfeiture,
But, touch'd with human gentleness and love,
Forgive a moiety of the principal,
Glancing an eye of pity on his losses,
That have of late so huddled on his back,
Enow to press a royal merchant down,
And pluck commiseration of his state
From brassy bosoms and rough hearts of flints,
From stubborn Turks, and Tartars never train'd
To offices of tender courtesy.
We all expect a gentle answer, Jew.

Shylock. I have possess'd your Grace of what I
purpose,
And by our holy Sabbath have I sworn
To have the due and forfeit of my bond:
If you deny it, let the danger light
Upon your charter and your city's freedom.
You'll ask me why I rather choose to have
A weight of carrion-flesh than to receive
Three thousand ducats: I'll not answer that:
But say it is my humour, is it answer'd?
What if my house be troubled with a rat,
And I be pleas'd to give ten thousand ducats
To have it ban'd? What, are you answer'd yet?
Some men there are love not a gaping pig;
Some that are mad if they behold a cat;
And others, when the bagpipe sings i' the nose,
Cannot contain their urine: for affection,
Master of passion, sways it to the mood
Of what it likes or loathes. Now for your
answer;

As there is no firm reason to be render'd
Why he cannot abide a gaping pig;
Why he a harmless necessary cat;
Why he a woollen bag-pipe; but of force
Must yield to such inevitable shame
As to offend, himself being offended;
So can I give no reason, nor I will not,
More than a lodg'd hate and a certain loathing
I bear Antonio, that I follow thus
A losing suit against him. Are you answer'd?

Bassanio. This is no answer, thou unfeeling man,
To excuse the current of thy cruelty.

Shylock. I am not bound to please thee with my
answers.

Bassanio. Do all men kill the things they do not
love?

Shylock. Hates any man the thing he would not
kill?

Bassanio. Every offence is not a hate at first.

Shylock. What, wouldst thou have a serpent sting
thee twice?

Antonio. I pray you, think you question with the
Jew:
You may as well go stand upon the beach,
And bid the main flood bate his usual height;
You may as well use question with the wolf,
Why he hath made the ewe bleat for the lamb;
You may as well forbid the mountain pines
To wag their high tops, and to make no noise,
When they are fretten with the gusts of heaven;
You may as well do any thing most hard,
As seek to soften that—than which what's
harder?—
His Jewish heart. Therefore, I do beseech you,
Make no moe offers, use no farther means,
But with all brief and plain conveniency
Let me have judgement, and the Jew his will.

Bassanio. For thy three thousand ducats here is six.

Shylock. If every ducat in six thousand ducats
  Were in six parts, and every part a ducat,
  I would not draw them, I would have my bond.

Duke. How shalt thou hope for mercy, rendering none?

Shylock. What judgement shall I dread, doing no wrong?
  You have among you many a purchas'd slave,
  Which, like your asses, and your dogs, and mules,
  You use in abject and in slavish parts,
  Because you bought them; shall I say to you,
  Let them be free, marry them to your heirs?
  Why sweat they under burthens? let their beds
  Be made as soft as yours, and let their palates
  Be season'd with such viands? you will answer
  'The slaves are ours:' so do I answer you:
  The pound of flesh which I demand of him
  Is dearly bought, is mine and I will have it.
  If you deny me, fie upon your law,
  There is no force in the decrees of Venice.
  I stand for judgement: answer, shall I have it?

Duke. Upon my power I may dismiss this court,
  Unless Bellario, a learned doctor,
  Whom I have sent for to determine this,
  Come here to-day.

Salerio.   My lord, here stays without
  A messenger with letters from the doctor,
  New come from Padua.

Duke. Bring us the letters, call the messenger.

Bassanio. Good cheer, Antonio! What, man, cour-
  age yet!
  The Jew shall have my flesh, blood, bones and all,
  Ere thou shalt lose for me one drop of blood.

Antonio. I am a tainted wether of the flock,
  Meetest for death; the weakest kind of fruit
  Drops earliest to the ground, and so let me:
  You cannot better be employ'd, Bassanio,
  Than to live still, and write mine epitaph.

   Enter Nerissa, dressed like a lawyer's clerk

Duke. Came you from Padua, from Bellario?
Nerissa. From both, my lord. Bellario greets your
  Grace.   *Presenting a letter*
Bassanio. Why dost thou whet thy knife so
  earnestly?
Shylock. To cut the forfeiture from that bankrupt
  there.
Gratiano. Not on thy sole, but on thy soul, harsh
  Jew.
  Thou mak'st thy knife keen; but no metal can,
  No, not the hangman's axe, bear half the
  keenness
  Of thy sharp envy. Can no prayers pierce thee?
Shylock. No, none that thou hast wit enough to
  make.
Gratiano. O, be thou damn'd, inexecrable dog,
  And for thy life let justice be accus'd!
  Thou almost mak'st me waver in my faith,
  To hold opinion with Pythagoras,
  That souls of animals infuse themselves
  Into the trunks of men: thy currish spirit
  Govern'd a Wolf, who hang'd for human
  slaughter,
  Even from the gallows did his fell soul fleet,
  And, whilst thou lay'st in thy unhallow'd dam,
  Infus'd itself in thee; for thy desires
  Are wolvish, bloody, starv'd, and ravenous.
Shylock. Till thou canst rail the seal from off my
  bond,

Thou but offend'st thy lungs to speak so loud:
Repair thy wit, good youth, or it will fall
To cureless ruin. I stand here for law.

Duke. This letter from Bellario doth commend
A young and learned doctor to our court:
Where is he?

Nerissa.   He attendeth here hard by,
To know your answer, whether you'll admit
him.

Duke. With all my heart: some three or four of
you
Go give him courteous conduct to this place;
Meantime the court shall hear Bellario's letter.
(*reads*) Your Grace shall understand that at
the receipt of your letter I am very sick, but in
the instant that your messenger came, in loving
visitation was with me a young doctor of Rome,
his name is Balthasar. I acquainted him with
the cause in controversy between the Jew and
Antonio the merchant; we turn'd o'er many
books together, he is furnish'd with my opinion,
which, bettered with his own learning, the
greatness whereof I cannot enough commend,
comes with him at my importunity, to fill up
your Grace's request in my stead. I beseech
you, let his lack of years be no impediment to
let him lack a reverend estimation, for I never
knew so young a body with so old a head. I
leave him to your gracious acceptance, whose
trial shall better publish his commendation.
You hear the learn'd Bellario, what he writes,
And here, I take it, is the doctor come.

Enter Portia for Balthasar

Give me your hand; come you from old
Bellario?

Portia. I did, my lord.
Duke.   You are welcome, take your place:
   Are you acquainted with the difference
   That holds this present question in the court?
Portia. I am informed throughly of the cause;
   Which is the merchant here? and which the
      Jew?
Duke. Antonio and old Shylock, both stand forth.
Portia. Is your name Shylock?
Shylock.   Shylock is my name.
Portia. Of a strange nature is the suit you follow,
   Yet in such rule, that the Venetian law
   Cannot impugn you as you do proceed.
   You stand within his danger, do you not?
Antonio. Ay, so he says.
Portia.   Do you confess the bond?
Antonio. I do.
Portia.   Then must the Jew be merciful.
Shylock. On what compulsion must I, tell me that.
Portia. The quality of mercy is not strain'd,
   It droppeth as the gentle rain from heaven
   Upon the place beneath: it is twice blest,
   It blesseth him that gives, and him that takes;
   'Tis mightiest in the mightiest, it becomes
   The throned monarch better than his crown;
   His sceptre shows the force of temporal power,
   The attribute to awe and majesty,
   Wherein doth sit the dread and fear of kings;
   But mercy is above this sceptred sway,
   It is enthroned in the hearts of kings,
   It is an attribute to God himself;
   And earthly power doth then show likest God's
   When mercy seasons justice. Therefore, Jew,
   Though justice be thy plea, consider this,
   That, in the course of justice, none of us
   Should see salvation: we do pray for mercy,

And that same prayer doth teach us all to
render
The deeds of mercy. I have spoke thus much
To mitigate the justice of thy plea,
Which if thou follow, this strict court of Venice
Must needs give sentence 'gainst the merchant
there.
Shylock. My deeds upon my head! I crave the
law;
The penalty and forfeit of my bond.
Portia. Is he not able to discharge the money?
Bassanio. Yes, here I tender it for him in the court,
Yea, twice the sum, if that will not suffice,
I will be bound to pay it ten times o'er,
On forfeit of my hands, my head, my heart:
If this will not suffice, it must appear
That malice bears down truth. And I beseech
you,
Wrest once the law to your authority,
To do a great right, do a little wrong,
And curb this cruel devil of his will.
Portia. It must not be, there is no power in Venice
Can alter a decree established:
'Twill be recorded for a precedent,
And many an error by the same example
Will rush into the state: it cannot be.
Shylock. A Daniel come to judgement! yea, a
Daniel!
O wise young judge, how I do honour thee!
Portia. I pray you, let me look upon the bond.
Shylock. Here 'tis, most reverend doctor, here it
is.
Portia. Shylock, there's thrice thy money offer'd
thee.
Shylock. An oath, an oath, I have an oath in
heaven:

Shall I lay perjury upon my soul?
No, not for Venice.
Portia.   Why, this bond is forfeit,
And lawfully by this the Jew may claim
A pound of flesh, to be by him cut off
Nearest the merchant's heart. Be merciful,
Take thrice thy money, bid me tear the bond.
Shylock. When it is paid according to the tenour.
It doth appear you are a worthy judge,
You know the law, your exposition
Hath been most sound: I charge you by the
    law,
Whereof you are a well-deserving pillar,
Proceed to judgement: by my soul I swear,
There is no power in the tongue of man
To alter me: I stay here on my bond.
Antonio. Most heartily I do beseech the court
To give the judgement.
Portia.   Why then, thus it is;
You must prepare your bosom for his knife.
Shylock. O noble judge! O excellent young man!
Portia. For the intent and purpose of the law
Hath full relation to the penalty,
Which here appeareth due upon the bond.
Shylock. 'Tis very true: O wise and upright judge,
How much more elder art thou than thy looks!
Portia. Therefore lay bare your bosom.
Shylock.   Ay, his breast,
So says the bond, doth it not, noble judge?
'Nearest his heart,' those are the very words.
Portia. It is so. Are there balance here to weigh
The flesh?
Shylock.   I have them ready.
Portia. Have by some surgeon, Shylock, on your
    charge,
To stop his wounds, lest he do bleed to death.

Shylock. Is it so nominated in the bond?

Portia. It is not so express'd, but what of that?
　'Twere good you do so much for charity.

Shylock. I cannot find it, 'tis not in the bond.

Portia. You, merchant, have you any thing to say?

Antonio. But little: I am arm'd and well prepar'd;
　Give me your hand, Bassanio, fare you well,
　Grieve not that I am fallen to this for you;
　For herein Fortune shows herself more kind
　Than is her custom: it is still her use
　To let the wretched man outlive his wealth,
　To view with hollow eye and wrinkled brow
　An age of poverty; from which lingering
　　penance
　Of such misery doth she cut me off.
　Commend me to your honourable wife,
　Tell her the process of Antonio's end,
　Say how I lov'd you, speak me fair in death;
　And when the tale is told, bid her be judge
　Whether Bassanio had not once a love.
　Repent but you that you shall lose your friend,
　And he repents not that he pays your debt;
　For if the Jew do cut but deep enough,
　I'll pay it instantly with all my heart.

Bassanio. Antonio, I am married to a wife
　Which is as dear to me as life itself,
　But life itself, my wife, and all the world,
　Are not with me esteem'd above thy life:
　I would lose all, ay, sacrifice them all
　Here to this devil, to deliver you.

Portia. Your wife would give you little thanks for
　　that,
　If she were by to hear you make the offer.

Gratiano. I have a wife, who I protest I love;
　I would she were in heaven, so she could
　Entreat some power to change this currish Jew.

Nerissa. 'Tis well you offer it behind her back,
The wish would make else an unquiet house.
Shylock. These be the Christian husbands; I have
a daughter;
Would any of the stock of Barrabas
Had been her husband rather than a Christian!
We trifle time, I pray thee pursue sentence.
Portia. A pound of that same merchant's flesh is
thine,
The court awards it, and the law doth give it.
Shylock. Most rightful judge!
Portia. And you must cut this flesh from off his
breast,
The law allows it, and the court awards it.
Shylock. Most learned judge, a sentence! Come,
prepare!
Portia. Tarry a little; there is something else.
This bond doth give thee here no jot of blood,
The words expressly are 'a pound of flesh:'
Take then thy bond, take thou thy pound of
flesh,
But in the cutting it, if thou dost shed
One drop of Christian blood, thy lands and
goods
Are by the laws of Venice confiscate
Unto the state of Venice.
Gratiano. O upright judge! Mark, Jew: O learned
judge!
Shylock. Is that the law?
Portia.   Thyself shalt see the act:
For, as thou urgest justice, be assur'd
Thou shalt have justice more than thou desirest.
Gratiano. O learned judge! Mark, Jew: a learned
judge!
Shylock. I take this offer then, pay the bond thrice
And let the Christian go.

Bassanio.   Here is the money.

Portia. Soft!

     The Jew shall have all justice; soft! no haste:
     He shall have nothing but the penalty.

Gratiano. O Jew! an upright judge, a learned
         judge!

Portia. Therefore prepare thee to cut off the flesh.
     Shed thou no blood, nor cut thou less nor more
     But just a pound of flesh: if thou tak'st more
     Or less than a just pound, be it but so much
     As makes it light or heavy in the substance,
     Or the division of the twentieth part
     Of one poor scruple, nay, if the scale do turn
     But in the estimation of a hair,
     Thou diest, and all thy goods are confiscate.

Gratiano. A second Daniel, a Daniel, Jew!
     Now, infidel, I have you on the hip.

Portia. Why doth the Jew pause? take thy
         forfeiture.

Shylock. Give me my principal, and let me go.

Bassanio. I have it ready for thee, here it is.

Portia. He hath refus'd it in the open court,
     He shall have merely justice and his bond.

Gratiano. A Daniel, still say I, a second Daniel!
     I thank thee, Jew, for teaching me that word.

Shylock. Shall I not have barely my principal?

Portia. Thou shalt have nothing but the forfeiture,
     To be so taken at thy peril, Jew.

Shylock. Why, then the devil give him good of it!
     I'll stay no longer question.

Portia.   Tarry, Jew,
     The law hath yet another hold on you.
     It is enacted in the laws of Venice,
     If it be prov'd against an alien
     That by direct or indirect attempts
     He seek the life of any citizen,

The party 'gainst the which he doth contrive
Shall seize one half his goods, the other half
Comes to the privy coffer of the state,
And the offender's life lies in the mercy
Of the Duke only, 'gainst all other voice.
In which predicament I say thou stand'st;
For it appears, by manifest proceeding,
That indirectly, and directly too,
Thou hast contriv'd against the very life
Of the defendant; and thou hast incurr'd
The danger formerly by me rehears'd.
Down therefore, and beg mercy of the Duke.
Gratiano. Beg that thou mayst have leave to hang
thyself:
And yet, thy wealth being forfeit to the state,
Thou hast not left the value of a cord;
Therefore thou must be hang'd at the state's
charge.
Duke. That thou shalt see the difference of our
spirit,
I pardon thee thy life before thou ask it:
For half thy wealth, it is Antonio's,
The other half comes to the general state,
Which humbleness may drive unto a fine.
Portia. Ay, for the state, not for Antonio.
Shylock. Nay, take my life and all, pardon not
that:
You take my house, when you do take the prop
That doth sustain my house; you take my life,
When you do take the means whereby I live.
Portia. What mercy can you render him, An-
tonio?
Gratiano. A halter gratis, nothing else for God's
sake.
Antonio. So please my lord the Duke, and all the
court,

To quit the fine for one half of his goods,
I am content; so he will let me have
The other half in use, to render it,
Upon his death, unto the gentleman
That lately stole his daughter:
Two things provided more, that, for this favour,
He presently become a Christian:
The other, that he do record a gift,
Here in the court, of all he dies possess'd,
Unto his son Lorenzo and his daughter.
Duke. He shall do this, or else I do recant
The pardon that I late pronounced here.
Portia. Art thou contented, Jew? what dost thou
say?
Shylock. I am content.
Portia.　　　　　　Clerk, draw a deed of gift.
Shylock. I pray you, give me leave to go from
hence;
I am not well, send the deed after me,
And I will sign it.
Duke.　　　　　Get thee gone, but do it.
Gratiano. In christening shalt thou have two god-
fathers:
Had I been judge, thou shouldst have had ten
more,
To bring thee to the gallows, not the font.
　　　　　　　　　　　　　Exit Shylock
Duke. Sir, I entreat you home with me to dinner.
Portia. I humbly do desire your grace of pardon,
I must away this night toward Padua,
And it is meet I presently set forth.
Duke. I am sorry that your leisure serves you
not.
Antonio, gratify this gentleman,
For, in my mind, you are much bound to him.
　　　　　　　　　　Exit Duke and his train

Bassanio. Most worthy gentleman, I and my
   friend
   Have by your wisdom been this day acquitted
   Of grievous penalties, in lieu whereof,
   Three thousand ducats, due unto the Jew,
   We freely cope your courteous pains withal.
Antonio. And stand indebted, over and above,
   In love and service to you evermore.
Portia. He is well paid that is well satisfied,
   And I, delivering you, am satisfied,
   And therein do account myself well paid;
   My mind was never yet more mercenary.
   I pray you, know me when we meet again,
   I wish you well, and so I take my leave.
Bassanio. Dear sir, of force I must attempt you
   further;
   Take some remembrance of us as a tribute,
   Not as a fee: grant me two things, I pray you,
   Not to deny me, and to pardon me.
Portia. You press me far, and therefore I will
   yield.
   Give me your gloves, I'll wear them for your
   sake;
   And, for your love, I'll take this ring from you:
   Do not draw back your hand, I'll take no more,
   And you in love shall not deny me this.
Bassanio. This ring, good sir, alas, it is a trifle!
   I will not shame myself to give you this.
Portia. I will have nothing else but only this,
   And now methinks I have a mind to it.
Bassanio. There's more depends on this than on
   the value.
   The dearest ring in Venice will I give you,
   And find it out by proclamation,
   Only for this I pray you pardon me.
Portia. I see, sir, you are liberal in offers;

You taught me first to beg, and now methinks
You teach me how a beggar should be answer'd.

Bassanio. Good sir, this ring was given me by my
wife,
And when she put it on, she made me vow
That I should neither sell, nor give, nor lose it.

Portia. That 'scuse serves many men to save their
gifts;
An if your wife be not a mad woman,
And know how well I have deserv'd this ring,
She would not hold out enemy for ever
For giving it to me. Well, peace be with you!

Exeunt Portia and Nerissa

Antonio. My Lord Bassanio, let him have the ring,
Let his deservings and my love withal
Be valued 'gainst your wife's commandment.

Bassanio. Go, Gratiano, run and overtake him,
Give him the ring, and bring him, if thou canst,
Unto Antonio's house: away! make haste.

Exit Gratiano

Come, you and I will thither presently,
And in the morning early will we both
Fly toward Belmont: come, Antonio. *Exeunt*

SCENE II

The same. A street

Enter Portia and Nerissa

Portia. Inquire the Jew's house out, give him this deed,
And let him sign it: we'll away to-night,
And be a day before our husbands home:
This deed will be well welcome to Lorenzo.

Enter Gratiano

Gratiano. Fair sir, you are well o'erta'en:
My Lord Bassanio upon more advice
Hath sent you here this ring, and doth entreat
Your company at dinner.
Portia.   That cannot be:
His ring I do accept most thankfully:
And so I pray you tell him: furthermore,
I pray you show my youth old Shylock's house.
Gratiano. That will I do.
Nerissa.   Sir, I would speak with you.
(*aside to Portia*) I'll see if I can get my husband's ring,
Which I did make him swear to keep for ever.
Portia. (*aside to Nerissa*) Thou mayst, I warrant.
We shall have old swearing
That they did give the rings away to men;
But we'll outface them, and outswear them too.
(*aloud*) Away! make haste: thou know'st where
I will tarry.
Nerissa. Come, good sir, will you show me to this
house?   *Exeunt*

ACT V

SCENE I

Belmont. Avenue to Portia's house

Enter Lorenzo and Jessica

Lorenzo. The moon shines bright: in such a night
as this,
When the sweet wind did gently kiss the trees,
And they did make no noise, in such a night
Troilus methinks mounted the Troyan walls,
And sigh'd his soul toward the Grecian tents,
Where Cressid lay that night.

Jessica.   In such a night
Did Thisbe fearfully o'ertrip the dew,
And saw the lion's shadow ere himself,
And ran dismay'd away.

Lorenzo.   In such a night
Stood Dido with a willow in her hand
Upon the wild sea banks, and waft her love
To come again to Carthage.

Jessica.   In such a night
Medea gather'd the enchanted herbs
That did renew old Æson.

Lorenzo.   In such a night
Did Jessica steal from the wealthy Jew,
And with an unthrift love did run from Venice,
As far as Belmont.

Jessica.   In such a night
Did young Lorenzo swear he lov'd her well,
Stealing her soul with many vows of faith,
And ne'er a true one.

Lorenzo.   In such a night
  Did pretty Jessica (like a little shrew)
  Slander her love, and he forgave it her.
Jessica. I would out-night you, did no body come;
  But, hark, I hear the footing of a man.

Enter Stephano

Lorenzo. Who comes so fast in silence of the
    night?
Stephano. A friend.
Lorenzo. A friend! what friend? your name, I
    pray you, friend?
Stephano. Stephano is my name, and I bring word
  My mistress will before the break of day
  Be here at Belmont: she doth stray about
  By holy crosses, where she kneels and prays
  For happy wedlock hours.
Lorenzo.   Who comes with her?
Stephano. None but a holy hermit and her maid.
  I pray you, is my master yet return'd?
Lorenzo. He is not, nor we have not heard from
    him.
  But go we in, I pray thee Jessica,
  And ceremoniously let us prepare
  Some welcome for the mistress of the house.

Enter Launcelot

Launcelot. Sola, sola! wo ha, ho! sola, sola!
Lorenzo. Who calls?
Launcelot. Sola! did you see Master Lorenzo?
  Master Lorenzo, sola, sola!
Lorenzo. Leave hollaing, man: here.
Launcelot. Sola! where? where?
Lorenzo. Here.
Launcelot. Tell him there's a post come from my
  master, with his horn full of good news: my
  master will be here ere morning.   *Exit*

Lorenzo. Sweet soul, let's in, and there expect
    their coming.
  And yet no matter: why should we go in?
  My friend Stephano, signify, I pray you,
  Within the house, your mistress is at hand,
  And bring your music forth into the air.

                   Exit Stephano
  How sweet the moonlight sleeps upon this
    bank!
  Here will we sit, and let the sounds of music
  Creep in our ears: soft stillness and the night
  Become the touches of sweet harmony.
  Sit, Jessica; look how the floor of heaven
  Is thick inlaid with patens of bright gold;
  There's not the smallest orb which thou be-
    hold'st
  But in his motion like an angel sings,
  Still quiring to the young-eyed cherubins;
  Such harmony is in immortal souls,
  But whilst this muddy vesture of decay
  Doth grossly close it in, we cannot hear it.

           Enter Musicians

  Come, ho, and wake Diana with a hymn!
  With sweetest touches pierce your mistress'
    ear,
  And draw her home with music.   *Music*
Jessica. I am never merry when I hear sweet
  music.
Lorenzo. The reason is, your spirits are attentive:
  For do but note a wild and wanton herd,
  Or race of youthful and unhandled colts,
  Fetching mad bounds, bellowing and neighing
    loud,
  Which is the hot condition of their blood,
  If they but hear perchance a trumpet sound,
  Or any air of music touch their ears,

You shall perceive them make a mutual stand,
Their savage eyes turn'd to a modest gaze,
By the sweet power of music: therefore the
  poet
Did feign that Orpheus drew trees, stones,
  and floods;
Since nought so stockish, hard, and full of rage,
But music for the time doth change his nature;
The man that hath no music in himself,
Nor is not mov'd with concord of sweet sounds,
Is fit for treasons, stratagems, and spoils,
The motions of his spirit are dull as night,
And his affections dark as Erebus:
Let no such man be trusted. Mark the music.

Enter Portia and Nerissa

Portia. That light we see is burning in my hall:
  How far that little candle throws his beams!
  So shines a good deed in a naughty world.
Nerissa. When the moon shone we did not see the
  candle.
Portia. So doth the greater glory dim the less;
  A substitute shines brightly as a king,
  Until a king be by, and then his state
  Empties itself, as doth an inland brook
  Into the main of waters. Music! hark!
Nerissa. It is your music, madam, of the house.
Portia. Nothing is good, I see, without respect:
  Methinks it sounds much sweeter than by day.
Nerissa. Silence bestows that virtue on it, madam.
Portia. The crow doth sing as sweetly as the lark,
  When neither is attended; and I think
  The nightingale, if she should sing by day,
  When every goose is cackling, would be
  thought
  No better a musician than the wren.
  How many things by season season'd are

To their right praise, and true perfection!
Peace, how the moon sleeps with Endymion,
And would not be awak'd.   *Music ceases*
Lorenzo.   That is the voice,
  Or I am much deceiv'd, of Portia.
Portia. He knows me as the blind man knows the
    cuckoo,
  By the bad voice.
Lorenzo.   Dear lady, welcome home.
Portia. We have been praying for our husbands'
    welfare,
  Which speed, we hope, the better for our
    words:
  Are they return'd?
Lorenzo.   Madam, they are not yet;
  But there is come a messenger before,
  To signify their coming.
Portia.   Go in, Nerissa;
  Give order to my servants that they take
  No note at all of our being absent hence,
  Nor you Lorenzo, Jessica nor you.
                  A tucket sounds
Lorenzo. Your husband is at hand, I hear his
    trumpet;
  We are no tell-tales, madam, fear you not.
Portia. This night methinks is but the daylight
    sick;
  It looks a little paler: 'tis a day,
  Such as the day is when the sun is hid.

   Enter Bassanio, Antonio, Gratiano, and their followers

Bassanio. We should hold day with the An-
    tipodes,
  If you would walk in absence of the sun.
Portia. Let me give light, but let me not be light,
  For a light wife doth make a heavy husband,

And never be Bassanio so for me:
But God sort all! You are welcome home, my
　lord.

Bassanio. I thank you, madam; give welcome to
　my friend.
This is the man, this is Antonio,
To whom I am so infinitely bound.

Portia. You should in all sense be much bound
　to him,
For, as I hear, he was much bound for you.

Antonio. No more than I am well acquitted of.

Portia. Sir, you are very welcome to our house:
It must appear in other ways than words,
Therefore I scant this breathing courtesy.

Gratiano. (*to Nerissa*) By yonder moon I swear
　you do me wrong;
In faith, I gave it to the judge's clerk,
Would he were gelt that had it, for my part,
Since you do take it, love, so much at heart.

Portia. A quarrel, ho, already! what's the matter?

Gratiano. About a hoop of gold, a paltry ring
That she did give me, whose posy was
For all the world like cutler's poetry
Upon a knife, 'Love me, and leave me not.'

Nerissa. What talk you of the posy or the value?
You swore to me when I did give it you,
That you would wear it till your hour of death.
And that it should lie with you in your grave:
Though not for me, yet for your vehement
　oaths,
You should have been respective and have
　kept it.
Gave it a judge's clerk! no, God's my judge,
The clerk will ne'er wear hair on 's face that
　had it.

Gratiano. He will, an if he live to be a man.

Nerissa. Ay, if a woman live to be a man.

Gratiano. Now, by this hand, I gave it to a youth,
A kind of boy, a little scrubbed boy,
No higher than thyself, the judge's clerk.
A prating boy, that begg'd it as a fee:
I could not for my heart deny it him.

Portia. You were to blame, I must be plain with you,
To part so slightly with your wife's first gift,
A thing stuck on with oaths upon your finger,
And so riveted with faith unto your flesh.
I gave my love a ring, and made him swear
Never to part with it, and here he stands;
I dare be sworn for him he would not leave it,
Nor pluck it from his finger, for the wealth
That the world masters. Now, in faith, Gratiano,
You give your wife too unkind a cause of grief:
An 'twere to me, I should be mad at it.

Bassanio. (*aside*) Why, I were best to cut my left hand off,
And swear I lost the ring defending it.

Gratiano. My Lord Bassanio gave his ring away
Unto the judge that begg'd it, and indeed
Deserv'd it too; and then the boy, his clerk,
That took some pains in writing, he begg'd mine,
And neither man nor master would take aught
But the two rings.

Portia.   What ring gave you, my lord?
Not that, I hope, which you receiv'd of me.

Bassanio. If I could add a lie unto a fault,
I would deny it; but you see my finger
Hath not the ring upon it, it is gone.

Portia. Even so void is your false heart of truth.
By heaven, I will ne'er come in your bed

Until I see the ring.

Nerissa.   Nor I in yours

Till I again see mine.

Bassanio.   Sweet Portia,

If you did know to whom I gave the ring,

If you did know for whom I gave the ring,

And would conceive for what I gave the ring,

And how unwillingly I left the ring,

When nought would be accepted but the ring,

You would abate the strength of your dis-

pleasure.

Portia. If you had known the virtue of the ring,

Or half her worthiness that gave the ring,

Or your own honour to contain the ring,

You would not then have parted with the ring.

What man is there so much unreasonable,

If you had pleas'd to have defended it

With any terms of zeal, wanted the modesty

To urge the thing held as a ceremony?

Nerissa teaches me what to believe;

I'll die for 't but some woman had the ring.

Bassanio. No, by my honour, madam, by my soul,

No woman had it, but a civil doctor,

Which did refuse three thousand ducats of me,

And begg'd the ring, the which I did deny him,

And suffer'd him to go displeas'd away;

Even he that had held up the very life

Of my dear friend. What should I say, sweet

lady?

I was enforc'd to send it after him,

I was beset with shame and courtesy,

My honour would not let ingratitude

So much besmear it. Pardon me, good lady,

For by these blessed candles of the night,

Had you been there, I think you would have

begg'd

The ring of me to give the worthy doctor.

Portia. Let not that doctor e'er come near my
  house,
  Since he hath got the jewel that I lov'd,
  And that which you did swear to keep for me,
  I will become as liberal as you,
  I'll not deny him any thing I have,
  No, not my body nor my husband's bed:
  Know him I shall, I am well sure of it:
  Lie not a night from home; watch me like
  Argus:
  If you do not, if I be left alone,
  Now, by mine honour, which is yet mine own,
  I'll have that doctor for my bedfellow.
Nerissa. And I his clerk; therefore be well
  advis'd
  How you do leave me to mine own protection.
Gratiano. Well, do you so: let not me take him
  then,
  For if I do, I'll mar the young clerk's pen.
Antonio. I am the unhappy subject of these quar-
  rels.
Portia. Sir, grieve not you, you are welcome not-
  withstanding.
Bassanio. Portia, forgive me this enforced wrong,
  And, in the hearing of these many friends,
  I swear to thee, even by thine own fair eyes,
  Wherein I see myself,—
Portia.   Mark you but that!
  In both my eyes he doubly sees himself;
  In each eye one: swear by your double self,
  And there's an oath of credit.
Bassanio.   Nay, but hear me:
  Pardon this fault, and by my soul I swear
  I never more will break an oath with thee.
Antonio. I once did lend my body for his wealth,
  Which, but for him that had your husband's
  ring,

Had quite miscarried: I dare be bound again,
My soul upon the forfeit, that your lord
Will never more break faith advisedly.
Portia. Then you shall be his surety. Give him
    this,
And bid him keep it better than the other.
Antonio. Here, Lord Bassanio, swear to keep this
    ring.
Bassanio. By heaven, it is the same I gave the
    doctor!
Portia. I had it of him: pardon me, Bassanio,
For, by this ring, the doctor lay with me.
Nerissa. And pardon me, my gentle Gratiano,
For that same scrubbed boy, the doctor's clerk,
In lieu of this last night did lie with me.
Gratiano. Why, this is like the mending of high-
    ways
In summer, where the ways are fair enough:
What, are we cuckolds ere we have deserv'd
    it?
Portia. Speak not so grossly. You are all amaz'd:
Here is a letter, read it at your leisure,
It comes from Padua, from Bellario:
There you shall find that Portia was the doctor,
Nerissa there her clerk: Lorenzo here
Shall witness I set forth as soon as you,
And even but now return'd; I have not yet
Enter'd my house. Antonio, you are welcome,
And I have better news in store for you
Than you expect: unseal this letter soon;
There you shall find three of your argosies
Are richly come to harbour suddenly:
You shall not know by what strange accident
I chanced on this letter.
Antonio.   I am dumb.
Bassanio. Were you the doctor, and I knew you
    not?

Gratiano. Were you the clerk that is to make me
  cuckold?
Nerissa. Ay, but the clerk that never means to
  do it,
  Unless he live until he be a man.
Bassanio. Sweet doctor, you shall be my bed-
  fellow;
  When I am absent, then lie with my wife.
Antonio. Sweet lady, you have given me life and
  living;
  For here I read for certain that my ships
  Are safely come to road.
Portia.   How now, Lorenzo?
  My clerk hath some good comforts too for you.
Nerissa. Ay, and I'll give them him without a fee.
  There do I give to you and Jessica,
  From the rich Jew, a special deed of gift,
  After his death, of all he dies possess'd of.
Lorenzo. Fair ladies, you drop manna in the way
  Of starved people.
Portia.   It is almost morning,
  And yet I am sure you are not satisfied
  Of these events at full. Let us go in,
  And charge us there upon inter'gatories,
  And we will answer all things faithfully.
Gratiano. Let it be so, the first inter'gatory
  That my Nerissa shall be sworn on, is,
  Whether till the next night she had rather stay
  Or go to bed now, being two hours to day:
  But were the day come, I should wish it dark,
  That I were couching with the doctor's clerk.
  Well, while I live, I'll fear no other thing
  So sore, as keeping safe Nerissa's ring. *Exeunt*